Tzemah Yoreh

So Compassionate it Hurts:
My Life as a Rabbi on the Spectrum

To Gina:
Happy reading!

Published by Modern Scriptures

http://www.modernscriptures.com

ISBN 979-8836444075

Printed in the United States of America

Cover illustration © 2022 by Peter Garceau

Book design by Tzemah Yoreh

I've massaged some of the names and dates of these events in
order to protect people's privacy. Otherwise, this actually
happened. Well, it mostly happened, because so much is
colored by perspective.

For Elisha, may you find your way

Acknowledgments

This was one of the easiest books to write and it was one of the hardest. It was the easiest because I've been writing a diary for twenty years and this is almost the same except for the omission of expletives (for the most part). It was the hardest because I had to think how I would present real-life people whom I love through the most compassionate lens of truth. I tried.

I would like to thank my spouse Aviva Richman who let me write this book and continues to inspire me to be a better person every single day. My parents continue to support my writing wherever it takes me. It would be so much harder to write and publish without their backing. My editors Andy Meisenheimer and Barbara Spindel made this book look like I imagined it in my dreams, I am very grateful for their vision.

I would like to also thank the UJA of New York for sponsoring a retreat for rabbis in June of 2021. So many members of the pastoral professions are suffering from serious burnout, and they gave us a wonderful and refreshing break, I started writing this book then.

Lastly, I wouldn't have written this book if it weren't for my beautiful boy Elisha, a smiling sphinx, who I hope one day will share his hopes and dreams with me.

Table of Contents

Preface

I am a congregational rabbi on the autism spectrum.

How is that possible? How can I thrive in a profession that is pastoral, that rewards extroversion, that seems mostly for those who intuitively grasp social dynamics? I can't understand my closest family members most of the time, let alone a room full of people whom I know only peripherally.

And yet I *have* thrived.

That is because along with the deficits of being on the spectrum, there are precious gifts that being neuroatypical bequeath me.

But, to be honest, it took me a while to find them.

I am a child of the '80s. Back then, there was simply no language around high-functioning autism. I knew I was different, but I couldn't describe how.

Something was always more than a little bit wrong, but I didn't know what it was. There were times I was happy, but I wouldn't say I had a happy childhood. I could never look others in the eye, and my body language was fairly wild. I shied away from most touch. I was so literal, and I was so lonely.

From a young age, I always sought to understand, but too often I was frustrated. As a child, I would reach for books on the higher shelf. I was a precocious reader, and my parents were academics. One of the volumes that changed my life was a book decoding body language for those who don't intuitively grasp it. I was finally able to pry open a window to understand other people, and more importantly to understand how others saw me.

As I grew older, there were other windows, the most important of which was poetry. The book on body language gave me some insight into people's minds, but poetry allowed me to go deeper.

I began to write poetry, and I began to write prayers. It was my poetry and prayers, their cadences of secular transcendence rooted in ancient texts, that led me to the rabbinate. My poetry drew the attention of others, and through them I found my community.

But it is one thing to find a community and it is altogether different to lead one. You can't lead through poetry, can you? My favorite poem in the world, by Avraham Ben Yitzhak, begins with these words (translated from the Hebrew):

> Happy are those who sow but do not reap
> For they have wandered far
> Happy are those who are generous
> And in their glorious youth have made the days lighter,
> Throwing their jewels
> as they traverse the story of their lives.

It is a poem about the greatest human beings, those who have enriched the world and touch everyone in passing; it is a poem about unfettered generosity. It is a poem about philosopher kings, who have achieved the second naïveté and live out their ideals at peace with the world.

This poem is one of my literary models for how to live life. I constantly ask myself if I am holding myself up to its ideals. The answer is no.

One of the central tenets of Humanist Judaism is the verse from Leviticus 19 that commands: "Love your neighbor as yourself." This tenet has been expressed in many different ways throughout history. Hillel the Elder said it encapsulated the entire Torah. James, the brother of Jesus, said that it was the royal law. Kant said it was the prime imperative, and there were and are countless thinkers all over the world who echo this, including the author of my favorite poem.

Those of a more skeptical bent may argue that the meaning of "Love your neighbor as yourself" in the Hebrew Bible is hardly reflective of a humanist philosophy. In the context of Leviticus, "Love your neighbor as yourself" meant: Love *him* and not her, since women are unequal to men. Love your neighbor *the Israelite*, but not the Canaanite whom you are commanded to destroy. Do not love your neighbor if he happens to be the idolater you are commanded to expunge from your midst, or the homosexual you are commanded to kill.

It is such a beautiful articulation, so profound and universal, but I doubt that many in the biblical period actually believed it in its entirety or lived up to it.

Humanity has progressed; today, more than at any other time in human history, many of us attempt to love our neighbors as ourselves. But I personally still do not think that I have lived up to this categorical imperative.

Have I truly treated my neighbor as I myself would wish to be treated?

Am I truly a "neighbor" to an African American woman? Have I considered the systemic racism that she endures constantly, her blocks as she seeks to educate her children and provide for her family, or even walk down the street in peace? I ask myself, if I truly loved and sought to understand transgender human beings who experience the world so differently, would I unthinkingly misgender people?

I am Jewish, and my family bears the scars of the Holocaust, yet how do I address the other anti-Semitism I am culpable of—anti-Muslim bias? Can I understand the harassment endured by a woman who wears a hijab?

Can I truly comprehend the other, whoever the other may be? Can I really put myself in someone else's shoes when I live in my world of privilege? I don't know if I can, but I am resolved that I shall continue in my attempt to do so, for that is the nature of a universal principle—we cannot entirely live up to it, only strive toward it.

That is what the gift of autism has taught me. I am so very different, and so I have striven so hard to understand others. Knowing that the world was not built for people like me, I have learned to recognize the obstacles others face as well.

I will always feel uncomfortable in social situations. Social interactions will continue to drain me, but now I work with that discomfort, which I recognize stems from trying and failing to understand the other, trying and failing to grasp their world. Trying to articulate my poetry and theirs. This is what autism has bequeathed me. This attempt is entirely genuine, without guile or pretense, and because people see this and appreciate it, I am able to connect to my community. It is why I am an effective rabbi.

But can I reach for something beyond effectiveness?

One of the gifts pastoral professions bestow upon those who practice them is the time to think deeply about ethics, and sometimes even to come up with some answers. A subject I have thought about deeply, in the last year in particular, is my responsibility as a community leader on the autism spectrum.

For many years I have kept the knowledge of my autism to myself. I always thought, this is who I am, and it is really no one's affair except my own, and no one will care anyway. But that is not actually true.

I'm writing this now, and sharing my experience, for my son Elisha.

At seven, Elisha inhabits a deeper band of the autism spectrum than I ever did. Will he ever have the words? Will he ever be able to advocate for himself and his needs? I do not know.

And if that is the case, I owe the beautiful human being who is my son to speak on his behalf. I want to understand him and what he needs to lead a fulfilling life, and I want to find a way to give it to him.

Because it is both my fault and my privilege that Elisha is autistic. Autism runs strong in the genes of my family. I went ahead and procreated with the full knowledge that I might have children like me, and Elisha is such a precious blessing, a sphinx whose puzzle I have not solved.

And so I will force myself to become even more eloquent, to turn over every rock, so that I can facilitate a meaningful and fulfilling life for my beautiful boy.

But there is more than my personal obligation to my son: There is my moral obligation to all my fellow journeyers on the spectrum. As a relatively articulate member of those who inhabit the various bands of the autism spectrum, I have the duty to speak up, to become an advocate because I can, while so many of us cannot.

I only realized this in the last few years. I only realized this when I became a rabbi of a community and the weight of responsibility began to rest upon my shoulders. And so it is time now. It is time to share my story with you and begin to advocate as best as I can.

PART ONE
COMPROMISING MATERIALS

Introduction

A common feature on my band of the spectrum is a stringent notion of fairness that is often very grating to others. Since some of us on the spectrum are less than adept at tone, volume, and formulation, we may sound pretty obnoxious to the non-initiated. Our rants get us kicked out of Facebook groups and shunned in polite society, and as children we often spent time in the principal's office because we yelled at our teacher for perceived capriciousness—or maybe that was just me!

Before I share my adventures as a rabbi and a pastor, perhaps I should explain exactly why I hollered at my eighth-grade teacher and regale you with some other stories from my life.

ii

I am the oldest of three siblings born to two Jewish studies professors who split their time between Toronto and Jerusalem. My brother is suave and charming, my sister is smart and dramatic; both are strikingly good-looking. I, however, was always the awkward misfit. I still am. I love my parents and my siblings, but many of my childhood memories make me wince. Something was definitely off.

When I was four, my brother knocked my mother's glasses off the bedside table and then told Momma that I did it. Momma proceeded to slap me, despite my protestations of innocence. My brother was two years old at the time and even then could lie like a politician. When I reflect on this episode, even four decades later, I still get angry. I get angry despite the fact that my mother was apologetic and the recognition that parents make mistakes. I don't think I forgave my mother her infraction until some ten years later, when I became really afraid that God was going to kill me on the Day of Atonement for being an unforgiving schmuck (I took God quite literally at certain points in my childhood). But why is that? Why do I still get angry about some small unfairness I endured as a young child? It seems so stupid.

My notions of fairness and unfairness are universal and unmalleable and haven't changed much since I was out of diapers. Right and wrong are vivid colors in my mind.

When I was six, I went to a French immersion public school in Toronto. Even then, Toronto was a diverse city of many immigrant groups, and there were a fair number of races and nationalities represented in my classroom. One little Greek girl was called Iphigenia (for the sacrificed Iphigenia of the classics), and I was told that she had the cooties. People would tease her and pull her hair and otherwise be as insufferably mean as only little kids can be. I appointed myself her protector and chased the bullies away. In retrospect, this was absolutely absurd because I was the shortest kid in my class and not even completely potty-trained. I was the frequent target of bullies myself. If anyone had the cooties, it was *me*. But I remember feeling that what she was enduring was so friggin unfair that someone had to speak up. I've always spoken up, and sometimes I've kicked, too.

When I was eight, my parents decided it was a good idea for their socially challenged eldest and the rest of the family to move to Israel for a year. From my perspective, this was great for language acquisition and absolutely nothing else. Israeli schools in the '80s were very violent places: Corporal punishment was still in practice, and a successful recess was when a child didn't go to the emergency room.

My brother was in first-grade at the time and was routinely picked on because of his large oval glasses. As an older brother, I had the responsibility to protect him, even though he was already demonstrating the advantages of greater height and weight, often beating me up himself. I weighed 53 pounds. So I went and kicked one of the bullies in the behind and ran away, and then I got caught. Next, I was hauled to the principal's office, where I was told by the bully that he had three older brothers in the school, and if I didn't watch it, they would teach me anew what pain was. The principal just sat quietly and smirked.

I remember this episode clearly. What it taught me was that authority is all well and good, but so often authority favors the status quo, and the status quo is often one where bullies reign unchallenged. As an eight-year-old, I could do little to change this. I realized very early on that only I could look out for myself.

When I returned to Canada, I enrolled in karate class and learned how to kick and punch and block, to protect myself from the repercussions brought on by my stringently loud voice. I was an A1 klutz, but I persevered. When I was 24, I got my black belt. No one picks on me anymore.

The only time I've ever used karate was in the New York subway 15 years ago, when a group of teenagers was stepping on my shopping bags. I politely asked them to be careful, but I was accused of dissing them and was threatened with physical violence. I used my karate voice and scared the living daylights out of them. They spit in my face and ran. I wiped it off, and when I got home, I threw up.

iii

When I was nine, I started yet another school, this time a secular Zionist establishment in northern Toronto. My parents were clearly a bit clueless when it came to socialization—throwing an autistic kid from one school to another ain't good for him! I got picked on, of course, this time for being "the guy with the beanie" when most of my classmates had pork sandwiches for lunch. I am no longer "the guy with the beanie"—I'm the guy with the awesome gray fedora—but that maltreatment still shines bright in my mind.

Flash forward thirty years to 2019, when I brought my eldest son, Lev, to an open house meant to attract members to my congregation, a secular establishment on the Upper West Side of New York. I told the audience that I didn't care whether he ended up ultra-Orthodox or an imam in suburban Riyadh, as long as he ended up being a mensch. That did not sit well with at least one prospective member, who informed me that my tolerance for anyone religious was unacceptable, especially those Hasids ("do you know the squalor they live in, rabbi?"), and that she would not recommend that her granddaughter attend our Sunday school. How is this remotely humanist? If we can't accept our Hasidic cousins, then how can we be tolerant of people of other cultures and faiths? Thirty years later, my kid is the guy with the beanie, and I am proud of him.

Two of the teachers at my new school in Toronto were of the capricious type, but number two, "Mrs. the Hag," was especially bad. I do not do well with authority wielded arbitrarily. I am generally uneasy in social situations, and this is especially true when a teacher will suddenly fling a detention in your face for blowing your nose too loudly. The typical interaction would involve her raising her voice at someone and meting out a punishment of unnecessary severity, my calling her on it in strident tones, the Hag going ape, and my ending up outside of the principal's office. This happened probably once a week, and after some time, seeing that she was making no headway with me, she called my mother. This was to no effect, as my mother supported me. Some parents would defend a rebellious teen just cuz, but I know that momma meant it.

Upon consultation with my parents, I bought a book on how to maintain control of a classroom. I wrapped it up real nice, and with a big smile on my face, presented it to her after graduation (not before graduation; credit me with basic survival instincts). Since you don't unwrap gifts until later, I didn't get to witness the violent eruption of the wicked witch of eighth-grade, but I am sure it was epic. Years later I was told that I turned into a school legend whose story was passed down from generation to generation. I do not feel any remorse about these actions. She had wielded her classroom authority like a dictator, and I could not live with that, just like I could not live with Iphigenia having the cooties.

iv

When I was sixteen, my parents shipped me and my brother off to boarding school in Israel. I was beyond angry at my parents' choice. Things were just starting to click for me in high school in Maple Leaf land. I had friends, which was never a given for me. I had just won the International Bible Contest, and so I was a minor celebrity. And there were even one or two girls I was interested in—there may have even been *a shared interest*. Girls would become very theoretical to me in the next three or four years because I didn't encounter any. The boys-only boarding school they chose was of the orthodox religious type where you studied rabbinic texts and ancient legal tomes for most of the day. My parents who taught these texts for a living at their local university thought it was vitally important that I acquire fluency in these texts, as well. I did not share their perspective.

Our day began at 6:40 with prayer, and ended at 8:30 pm, then there was homework. Afterwards, we could read books with most of the good parts crossed out, or we could dance to the tune of biblical verses, or we could go to bed and cry ourselves to sleep (that's what I usually chose).

What made this school into a true hellhole, however, was the pederasty. The head of this 'venerable' institution would actually get convicted a few years later after I left for the sexual abuse of my classmates. It was probably just an accident of fate that he didn't touch me, though it could have been the vigilance regarding sexual abuse instilled in me by mother, or maybe it was my pimples and back brace. I don't know and I shudder at the what-ifs.

The primary reason my parents sent me to that school was because my brother needed to get out of the house; there were no more rules to break at home, and he needed to break things elsewhere. But *I* didn't need to get out of the house. *I* was just fine where I was. They didn't want my brother to think they'd abandoned him though, and so they sent me for the ride. After one year there I begged my parents to get me out of this hellish environment. Nope.

What my parents did made sense to them, they saw it as an act of love, but to me it seemed decidedly immoral. According to Kant, you must never use another human being as a means toward an end. You should love your neighbor and your son for themselves and as themselves.

I understood this principle intuitively, had understood it from a very young age, and at 16 I was finally beginning to acquire the words and the logical sophistication to articulate my deep dissatisfaction. At 16, most of those words would have been expletives.

Years later, when I was 32, eating dinner with my new wife at my parents' house, I asked my father whether he was excited at the prospect of grandchildren. My father said no because he was Kantian and didn't see me as a means toward an end. I thought this was entirely obnoxious, and I lost it. When he asked me to pass the water, I said no, you are a Kantian, you should not view me as a means toward slaking your thirst. What did my father know of Kant after sending me to that boarding school?

V

One silver lining of boarding school was that I was exempt from math classes. I have the typical Aspie gift for figures, and I had finished with high school math the year before. I used the time off to do my brother's math tests for him, which for some reason the teacher let him take to his room. The fluctuation in his grades from 40 to 100 and back again was noticeable enough that even a teacher with cheater blinders could not fail to notice it, so we stopped that in the second trimester there. We weren't caught, though we should have been.

You might ask why I was okay with cheating. Well, I made an excuse for myself, that my brother was having a hard time away from home and that any way I could help him was fine. A psychologist would probably say that I was acting out my aggression against authority any way I could, and they would be right, but I also didn't think it was fair that my brother, who was not strong at math, should be thrown into the deep end of a subject he did not excel at in a foreign language to boot.

It may surprise you, considering all my high-minded talk about morality, but I am a slippery Slytherin (and, yes, a Harry Potter fan). I have a very healthy disregard for rules that don't make sense to me. So did Severus Snape, and he also had Asperger's, according to the Internet. And he saved Harry Potter's life.

So there.

vi

College transformed me from an idealistic teenager to a cynical adult in a few years—I guess that is what college is supposed to do. At first, I was loving every moment. I took 13 courses for credit in my first semester, and that did not include the courses I was auditing! I was interested in everything, and since I had no friends, and wasn't likely to attract many women since I had not mastered personal hygiene, I spent my time from dawn to dusk studying. My grades were free-ride type of grades, and I maintained that high average throughout college.

When did my idealism turn into cynicism? When I was stabbed in daylight by Brutus—and by Brutus I mean Professor Saul.

Lucky for me, I wasn't female, otherwise I shudder to think of what my relationship with this smooth player might have been. The man was a notorious womanizer, the type that was largely tolerated throughout the 20th century.

It started with an argument I had in Professor Saul's office regarding climax and tension. And by climax, I mean the climax of a story of a war between gods. I argued that the moment of highest tension right before the explosion of death should be seen as such, and he argued that the moment *right afterward* was more accurately the climax.

I lost the argument with the slimy man who knew a lot more about climaxes than I did and got a B. I'd always thought that if you mounted a convincing argument, that it would be respected and rewarded in the holy halls of the university. I thought that wholesale regurgitation was a high school thing, but apparently not. I quickly adapted, and henceforth my grade point average was 4.3. The climax of my idealism had obviously passed.

My idealistic self said, don't worry, dude, when you get to grad school, everything will be different, and your genius will be hailed by all. My idealistic self was stupid, but you must forgive me, I am an academic brat after all. One of the deep ironies of academic writing—which only dawned on me slowly—is that the more uncertain a case is, the more forcefully you are to present your argument. The reason for this is that "speculative" is the ultimate pejorative in my field, reserved for only the malodorous garbage produced by third-rate academics. What ends up happening is that you consciously overrepresent your case, especially when your case is flimsy. In other words, you lie.

I cannot abide by lies.

I remember at one particular conference, when I admitted I was engaging in speculative thinking regarding the mystery of the red heifer, they piled up on me like I was a quarterback for the Cleveland Browns. When you speculate, you can dream big and advance your field—that was my opinion, at least—but I no longer wish to advance my field. Now the writing I undertake in the fields of my choice is for onanistic purposes only; it is because I enjoy language and words with an almost sensual pleasure that I continue prodding at the Bible with my pincers.

The reason I finally left academia and will likely not return is the violence of academic "dialogue." My alma mater, Hebrew University, combines the worst of the German academic tradition and Israeli culture. In my first Bible course,

Introduction to Bible, I saw my professor tear down a student's claims regarding the inviolate sanctity of the Pentateuch. It was great fun. It was also a preview to the culture of argument (or more accurately knife-fighting) that was such a big part of my academic experience. I was very good at it. I was adept at marshaling arguments spurious and otherwise against my interlocutors and wielding them like weapons. For the first time in my life, the strident tone of voice that is a feature of my neural wiring served me well.

The turning point came when I blithered and blathered at high volume regarding a minor philological point during the Q&A portion of a lecture delivered at the Association for Jewish Studies. I was called out for my behavior by two people whom I don't especially like, which heightened the humiliation. Realizing I'd behaved poorly, I publicly apologized for my tone. I left town the next day, and I have not returned to that particular conference since. What I remember most vividly is the feeling of utter disgust with myself, and a vow never to speak that way in academic debates ever again. Henry Kissinger once said that the reason that university politics is so vicious is because the stakes are so small. Deep in my psyche, I knew that the arguments I was having with people were of little import. As much as I enjoy academic knife-fighting, it was a small pleasure of a small man. I wanted to be better than that.

vii

Having completed my doctorate in less than one and a half years, and having been regurgitated by my university without a job and without any prospects, despite the high opinion I had of myself, I became a cynic. The word cynic comes from the Greek *kunikos*, which means *dog*. At times the only thing it seemed like I inherited from the university was a heightened ability to bark. I applied my cynicism to everything, and one day it dawned on me that the words I had been saying at synagogue—which, like so much of Jewish scripture, I knew by heart—were anathema to me. I didn't believe in God, nor the world of values reflected in a liturgy composed two thousand years ago.

And so I submitted my resignation to heaven, sold my soul on eBay and became an atheist—not really. But I was deeply disappointed in myself for not having realized all of this sooner. I had been mouthing these words for many years, but only now did I finally realize the discrepancy between my values and those in traditional prayer. I remember the moment, because in that instant going to traditional synagogues became utterly unbearable. My ethical compass, wired so deeply into my psyche, would not let me suspend disbelief even for a moment. Honestly, sometimes I wish that I could have; it would have made my life so much easier, preventing my alienation from mainstream Judaism. But I just couldn't say what I didn't believe was true, even if some of my best friends were saying it. I just couldn't.

I've spent the 18 or so years since trying to heal this rupture. I've written hundreds of thousands of words of liturgical rumination, and I still haven't found my way back. But wandering in the wilderness, I have found others like me, and we have created some beautiful moments.

I did leave another desert in those years: the desolation of being alone. In late 2006 I met my future wife, Aviva, after I corrected her Hebrew grammar. Today she is a religious leader, the first woman to head a traditional yeshiva, and is correcting my social faux pas.

viii

My marriage is a mystery that I still don't understand. Why would someone neurotypical marry me? I am a few standard deviations from normal. It's not that I lack self-esteem—I have plenty of that—but why would a dog marry a cat? I have been trying to figure this out ever since my wife proposed and I said yes, and maybe even before that, when we were dating. Back then, I always had an uneasy feeling that she was "slumming" and would soon tire of me. She hasn't, and we have been married for 14 years.

In many ways my marriage followed an idealized trajectory. I became very good friends with my wife before we started dating, and that is how I'd always envisioned it. We met at synagogue—a fairly generic meeting story as that goes. Single people often go to synagogue in order to meet mates. It was so normal, and so utterly unexpected. It's like in the books, except this was real life. Aviva had been studying abroad post-college and was a whiz at rabbinic literature. I was doing a postdoc at Ben Gurion University and was pretending to run a synagogue in Jerusalem. She remembers how I corrected her on a minor grammatical point while she was chanting from the Torah scroll, and I remember how she later came up to me at a party and said, "Hi, I'm Aviva." No woman had ever approached me at a party and introduced herself. To be fair, I attended very few parties. I don't remember why I was at that one. My usual activity at parties was to sit in a corner, drink wine from a disposable cup, and glower, which is not conducive to meaningful interaction with anyone, let alone potential romantic partners. Sometimes, if I'd had six drinks, I could actually converse. It took that much—I am cursed with a very high alcohol tolerance.

I then began noticing Aviva popping up in various locations, most often at an advanced rabbinics class I was taking. She was the only woman there, which impressed me, and then we became friends. One day we were walking together, and I asked her whether she would like to be more than friends, and she asked me what would be different, and I said we'd be holding hands right now instead of walking side by side, and she said she would consider it. The next day she'd considered it, and then she kissed me. And that was that.

But why? The Book of Proverbs says:

> *There are three things that are entirely beyond me, and four that I do not understand: the way of an eagle in the sky, the way of a snake on a rock, the way of a ship on the high seas, and the way of a man with a woman.*

Presumably the author of Proverbs was neurotypical—though I don't know—but even he had difficulty understanding how this worked. I, an "Aspie," have a further degree of removal, so women and romance are even more of a mystery to me than to a neurotypical male.

Aviva grew up with a very deliberate hyper-analytic father, who was nothing like me but perhaps gave her a more nuanced idea of the range of human beings out there. In school she would always look for the people who were left out and try to befriend them. I was often left out, so maybe her initial attraction to me made sense. I also had a black belt in martial arts and scored very well on standardized tests, but who gives a rat's behind about those things?

I understand why I was attracted to her. She was a tall, nice-looking woman who didn't tell me to go to hell. That was a first. She was soft-spoken with a gently ironic sense of humor, and she was compassionate. She was also intellectually driven—not in the academic sense, she didn't really care about degrees and such—but in the much rarer "I am curious and want to learn more" kind of way.

It is one thing to be attracted to someone and another thing altogether to build a life with them. The liberal English-speaking social group of Jerusalem, which we were both part of, was shocked that we'd gotten together. What was this good religious girl doing with this atheist weirdo who was sometimes fun to talk to because he had a certain skill at ranting, but otherwise not worthy of much attention?

Apparently, Aviva decided to find out what I was worth. She stayed in Jerusalem for another year, and at the end of her time there she proposed to me, though to be fair she kind of signaled she was ready when she started ring-shopping, so it wasn't unexpected.

But I still do not know what she sees in me, and I haven't really asked, in case whatever spell I cast on her breaks and she dumps me on the street corner.

We are now many years into our marriage and have four boys. We've thrown heteronormativity to the winds. I've stayed at home with our boys so much more than she has, while she got ordained, finished her doctorate, and became an executive at her institution. I think I got the better end of the bargain, since I love to spend time with the little kiddos, and I saw her success as mine, because of how I enabled it.

Living with someone neuroatypical can be challenging, however, and the grand bargain I struck with Aviva shouldn't obfuscate that. I think that the most difficult aspect of our marriage is that I judge Aviva by a higher standard than I do pretty much anyone else in the world. I do that because I think she is that awesome, better than anyone else in the world, in fact—certainly better than me—but it leads to quite a bit of tension.

I am anal-retentive around timing. It is part of my deep attraction to patterns, which calm me, as is the case with so many autistic people. If Aviva is ten minutes late coming home, I have difficulty with that, even though I know she tries her best. It doesn't help matters that she is aspirational regarding the time she is likely to arrive home and is almost always late. I try telling that to myself, but it is hard, and sometimes I yell.

Aviva always thinks I am yelling, and that is because I am. Well, at least relative to her. I do not know how to modulate. My mother rode me hard about that as a kid, so any time Aviva brings up my tone of voice or my voice's decibels, I become defensive. Yelling does not connote anger for me, and that is something Aviva doesn't totally get.

I like to think, though, that my being on the spectrum sometimes helps our relationship. When Aviva was pregnant with our first child, she lost a necklace that she'd chosen for herself and that I'd bought. I didn't just buy it, I went into debt to buy it, and she loved that necklace. She'd taken it off when she was doing pregnancy yoga a few weeks before our son was born. She was swelling up like a Vienna sausage and it made sense to take off the necklace and put it down somewhere, just not in a studio where people go in and out all day. People like shiny things, and someone unscrupulous apparently decided to keep that exquisitely wrought necklace. I could have gotten apoplectically angry considering the cost of that trinket. But I was merely annoyed. I have never viewed possessions or money as anything but a means toward an end. I had proven how much I valued Aviva by giving her that gift, and it had served its purpose.

I also recognized that Aviva's mind was undergoing a profound rewiring catalyzed by pregnancy hormones; as a result, she was not attuned toward logistics. I called it 'pregnancy brain' until Aviva told me to shut up and never say that again. But I didn't mean that as an insult. It was my acknowledgment of the plasticity of our minds, of how we can change who we are in profound ways. My own commitment to deliberately change my brain's wiring so that I would be able to function in a neurotypical world has been core to my identity ever since childhood.

Ultimately, though, I think what makes our marriage work is that we are both mediators—we know how to compromise—and even when we don't compromise, we know how to live with differences of opinion. When Aviva writes lyrical sermons about God, which she does often, I read in between the lines and appreciate the richness of her thought. When I get to God, I just think of him as the literary god character. Our children hear different and hopefully thoughtful voices on how to celebrate their Judaism, and we are okay with that.

And yet despite all of this I don't know how she lives with me. I raise my voice way too often, and she doesn't deserve it at all, because she has never had an ill intention in her life. I expect her to be some sort of wonder woman who can be an attentive mother, cook wonderful meals, earn most of the money, and still have time to interact with me, and when she can't live up to this idealized crap of mine, I get disappointed and angry. I experience touch very differently than most human beings, and I often shy away from physical contact with her, I know that is hard and she doesn't deserve that. I try to write her beautiful poetry, but my imagery is sometimes too complicated she cannot understand it, and she gets frustrated.

My wife has been somewhat bemused at my Aspie awakening. I told her about being on the spectrum before we got married, as I felt that she should know. But we didn't really discuss it much until a couple of years ago. As I said in the introduction, my attitude until recently was "it ain't nobody's business except my own." But then, she read an article that I wrote for thehill.com about being a rabbi on the spectrum and the gifts that autism has bequeathed me (the article that led to this book). And she gazed at me for a long moment and said, "That is why I married you."

ix

The same year I met my wife, I also got my first three professional breaks in the space of a couple of weeks. I got a job offer, a postdoc, and a second postdoc. Had these come any later, I would not have written this book, because I would have been an accountant.

I came to the United States for a job (everyone does eventually), and I was unfortunately eligible to vote pretty much immediately. Doesn't really seem fair, but there it is. My mother's ancestors had bequeathed me this right having first come here from Ireland before the War of Independence. I was supposed to vote for either Barack Obama or John McCain, and if I chose John McCain, I would have to keep it to myself so as not to get fired from my place of work. I had no strong opinions about American politics at the time. My aversion to George W. Bush and his Republicans was mostly because on Bush Junior's final visit to Jerusalem, he ruined my wife's plan to propose to me in the way she wanted to because men on horses blocked off all kinds of streets. Not really a sound basis upon which to choose the leader of the free world.

So I decided to read a bit of history, and based on the recommendation of *Good Will Hunting*, I started with Howard Zinn's *A People's History of the United States*. It would knock my socks off, according to the endorsement of the fictional boy genius Will Hunting, whom I absurdly identified with. My socks stayed on, but I enjoyed the book. And then Howard Zinn, who I was surprised to find out was still alive, endorsed Ralph Nader for president. On a whim I watched a documentary about this iconoclastic politician called *An Unreasonable Man.* I loved it, and I ended up voting for him. It turns out it was an unfortunate family tradition.

My grandmother had voted for Nader in 2000 in Florida to spite her daughters, two of whom had converted to Judaism. She considered Nader an anti-Semite because of his Lebanese heritage and wanted to stick it to "Sore Loserman" (the Gore/Lieberman ticket). Enough people like my grandmother determined the fate of the 2000 election. In 2008, to be fair, she recalls voting for "that Indian guy," who I assume was Obama, though my grandmother wasn't at the apotheosis of her mental acuity at the time. Forgivable, considering she was in her tenth decade of life.

I also thought that politicians all belonged in the Judeo-Christian version of hell because as a group they were the most venal, corrupt, money-grubbing group of people I've ever had the misfortune of not meeting. What do you call five thousand politicians at the bottom of the ocean? A good start.

I loved the idea of not compromising, and I also hated the rhetoric around the legalization of gay marriage at that time. The turning point for me was during the vice-presidential debate between Joe Biden and Sarah Palin, when both candidates agreed that gay marriage should not be legal. And I could not stand it. I could not compromise or be "reasonable" on this, and so I voted for an unreasonable man, a guy who as far as I could tell stood for something and did not belong at the bottom of the sea.

X

I lasted in my job for only two years. You remember 2008, when stocks became worthless and millions of worthy people lost their jobs. I was one of those worthy people.

It was the worst thing that had ever happened to me; it was the best thing that had ever happened to me. I taught Hebrew Bible at a conservative movement rabbinical school, but I was also an out-of-the-closet heretic. I had already written and disseminated "atheist feminist" prayerbooks and other such compositions that would have had me burned at the stake in another day and age. Before I was hired, the dean called me into his office and asked, "So what kind of atheist are you?" Clearly there was a right answer and a wrong answer to the question. I answered wrong and got the job.

I answered wrong because I pandered: I told him what he wanted to hear, and I find pandering to be disingenuous. It was a moment of dishonesty, and I don't even know if he believed me, but he was willing to go along. Later, he told everyone that the reason I lost my job was not because of the economic downturn; it was because of my attempts to indoctrinate the students to accept the gospel of atheism. I have never indoctrinated anyone in my life. I wouldn't know how if I tried. Clearly, I was not cut out for the slippery politics of academia. In truth, I am not cut out for any politics whatsoever.

In retrospect, this termination was a blessing in a disguise. It helped clarify for me the type of professions I was suited for, and they were sadly not many—politics are everywhere. For the next eight years I would search for a sessile profession that would not compromise me ethically and would allow me to munch blueberries for most of the day in front of a computer screen while bouncing babies on a knee.

I've tried my hand at writing. I've written over 40 books— great books, mind you, with steamy titles like *Why Abraham Murdered Isaac*, but books that no one reads. I tried karate—I had a third-degree black belt after all—but I am not cut out to teach middle-schoolers martial arts. The girls in the class laughed at me (I don't think they've stopped since I was a middle-schooler myself). I tried being an adjunct and teaching at various institutions in three different countries, but that paid worse than fast-food joints and was more degrading. In desperation, I even earned a second PhD. My wife was earning her first at the time, and we had two kiddos, so we moved to Toronto for a bit to be with my family so they could pretend to help.

I finished my second PhD quite quickly for the same reason I finished my first quickly. I didn't really like what I was doing. My reemergence on the academic stage got my parents' hopes up that I would move to Canada and become a prof. I've tried to dash my parents' hopes many times in the most explicit of terms, employing many four-letter words, but they still think that I am the savior of the humanities. Parents are so often deluded about their children.

The only job that I had any sustained luck at was freelancing. I translated and edited, and I even officiated at a few weddings, but when child number three came, my wife insisted that I find more steady work. I wasn't in a position to disagree; she had just borne and nursed three children and I had not.

Not that I was a sloth. I was a stay-at-home dad who spent lots and lots of quality time with my beautiful kiddos, and I had pushed, prodded, and enabled my wife to finish her PhD and assume an executive position as a leader of a Jewish organization. Her success was mine, but I needed some of my own successes too.

xii

For a long time I had fiddled and twiddled with the idea of becoming a rabbi. The first time was in my twenties, when I almost got Orthodox ordination, but ultimately I just couldn't lie well enough to myself. I told my teacher that it would not be intellectually honest or sustainable to say to anyone seeking my advice, "I find the legal paradigm of Talmudic-based Jewish law antiquated and immoral, but if you need a ruling, this is what it would be…" There was my stupid, baked-in moral compass rearing its reliable head again.

Years later, as I was on the way out from academia the first time around, a long article about my non-theistic liturgical projects appeared in two Jewish newspapers. It was entitled "No God No Problem." Baby, was it a problem. My wife's attempt at securing employment was severely compromised because I was a threat to impressionable children who would be seduced by my logical fallacies. I decided to make some lemonade from these lemons: When the head of the International Institute for Secular Humanist Judaism contacted me to try out his rabbinical school, I accepted. Four years later, I finished my studies and became a rabbi. Mind you, I was planning to do very little with this degree except roll it out at dinner parties and bar mitzvahs, but it did add authority to my rewriting of prayers that non-theists could say without cringing. The only really worthwhile thing I did with my rabbinical degree until recently was help a fair number of people adopt Judaism as their affiliation. And then this job came up at the only humanist congregation in New York City, and for some reason I got it.

I haven't quite decided whether my success at being a congregational rabbi is because of my autism or in spite of it. Why don't you read some more and tell me?

Part Two
A Spectrum of Gifts

The Gift of Truth

I cannot lie.

Okay, so that is not exactly true. I cannot lie *well*, for I have not adequately mastered the body language that those accomplished at duplicity so skillfully employ.

This is of course part of a greater complex of common autistic character traits. I am also very literal.

I could learn how to lie, I suppose, but considering that I do not foresee a late career in politics, lawyering, or other forms of skullduggery, what's the point?

I can't say that I am particularly sad that I lack these skills. Being inherently truthful has proven to be a great boon as a rabbi.

But sometimes it is damned inconvenient.

Like the time when I needed a security clearance in my twenties and I was asked whether I'd ever smoked marijuana. I could have said no, or better yet claimed that I did not inhale. But I didn't. Come on, dude, almost everyone of my age had at least tried ganj, and many indulged in it profusely. It was such a stupid question. But stupid questions sometimes require stupid answers. The expectation is that you lie. In fact, if you are a compulsive truth-teller, there are certain positions in this world you should not occupy.

The powers that be made a good choice. I didn't get my security clearance.

Philosophers have emptied their fountain pens speaking for and against white lies, and knowing myself, I am sure that if I had the capacity to be mendacious in any way, shape, or form, I'd engage in tortured analyses of the ethics of this societal lubricant and never get anything said or done. So it is actually quite lucky that I have no ability to tell a lie.

It is also freeing in surprising ways.

Like the time I came back from Amsterdam and a cop confronted me in the airport, asking if I had ingested any illegal substances while I was there and if I had by any chance brought some back with me, and by the way how would I like to decorate my jail cell? I just burst out in genuine laughter and asked him if I had anything illegal on me, did he really think I would tell him?

He did not enjoy that response and I was searched, but he didn't find anything on me. I would never have done anything so ill-advised.

Compulsive truth-telling probably had a greater influence on my career trajectory than I'd like to acknowledge. It made me a rabbi instead of a professor.

You see, I have two PhD's in the humanities, so obviously I've at least contemplated other paths.

The cesspool of academic politics I had been exposed to as the child of offbeat professors put me off, though not enough, apparently.

I submitted my doctorate in Bible to the Hebrew University of Jerusalem when I was 24 years old. I looked like I was 19. I had been enrolled in the PhD program for 17 months.

What a genius, people would say about me, sometimes even within my hearing. What an idiot, I would mutter to myself years later.

The reason I finished my doctorate so fast had nothing to do with my inborn talent, but rather with the burning hatred I had for the institution and many of its professors. Hatred is sometimes a great motivator.

Don't get me wrong, I loved what I was studying and the university facilitated that. I got very good grades—why the hell are you not in law school at Harvard type grades.

You also have to understand, I had no friends. I was in a back brace that made me look like a robot, and I hadn't yet mastered the mystery of personal hygiene, so I smelled like the restrooms at Grand Central after the food court was closed for salmonella.

I was so innocent. I had bought in to the idealism my father and mother had spouted at me all my life about academic meritocracy. They convinced me that my original thinking and native intelligence would pave my way to the gilded halls of the most prestigious universities. Bullshit.

As in so many professions, it's not what you know, it's who you know. Idealists are begging at street corners or adjuncting for fifteen bucks per hour. And, by the way, those are not mutually exclusive.

I chose an advisor whose ideas appealed to me. He was not senior. He was not on the make. He was socially and politically clueless. He loved exploring ideas that sometimes were in the mainstream and sometimes qualified him for the equivalent of the academic loony bin. I liked him.

In other words, I was stupid.

Well, perhaps stupid is not the right adjective—I did, after all, finish my PhD in 17 months. Naïve is probably the better term, and also the nicer one.

In hindsight, what I appreciated about academia is the genuine search for truth, without a point system attached to it.

ii

My preoccupation with truth is what led me to become a Jewish humanist. One of the values we emphasize most is "saying it like it is."

That strikes a deep chord in my depths. I acknowledge that transvaluation—or going beyond the simple meaning of words—is a way to appreciate the ancient texts and prayers of yesteryear. Such is my spouse's way. It is not mine. I love Judaism's ancient texts, but if the primary meaning of an ancient text does not conform with my values, I can appreciate it aesthetically or literarily, but I cannot use it as prayer. Thus, I have been driven to write and write in order to find words that do have meaning for me.

In another chapter of this book, I discuss the poetry that emerges from the synergy of truth and literalness. Here I want to speak for a moment about how I've used this proclivity in my interactions as a rabbi.

Being a truth-teller has helped me be a good mediator. When I present one person's actions or speech to another person, I strive to present them truthfully and compassionately. If a purely hypothetical Ruth screamed at Isaac and called him a misogynist because he defended the donning of a hijab in public spaces in American cities as a valid expression of female religiosity instead of patriarchal oppression, what would I do?

Inwardly, I would perhaps utter some expletives regarding my lot in life, but outwardly I would present a pleasant countenance. Over the years I've perfected the bland face.

I would first talk to Ruth about her passion for women's rights and validate it. I could have mansplained to her that yelling in a public forum was inappropriate. Both statements would have been true. But I see the former as more pertinent, because it speaks to the underlying truth of Ruth's experience. She is yelling because she feels so strongly about women's rights, which is a wonderful thing, and this is what I choose to emphasize at first. I would then ask her to consider the expressed views of women in hijabs who want to practice their religion as they see fit, at the same time conceding that there are probably many women who don hijabs who may not wish to but are doing it because of family pressure; still, we probably should not generalize regarding all Muslim American women. I would present her with these findings through articles and graphs and try to convince her of this. Hopefully, by this point, Ruth would have agreed that yelling at Isaac and calling him a misogynist was inappropriate—perhaps she would have even agreed to apologize—but even if that were not the case, the next time she would not be as quick to yell.

You see, the truth is like a jewel of many facets. I will always choose the facet that highlights the good in a particular situation. I don't ignore the negativity inherent in raising one's voice in anger. The very fact that I was addressing the situation with Ruth implies that it is concerning. This hypothetical Ruth is smart enough to understand that. One hopes that she would go on to acknowledge this and apologize, but she would do so not from a place of shame, but from a place of validation.

What about Isaac? I would ask this hypothetical Isaac how he was doing after this unfortunate interaction with Ruth and express regret for the outburst. I wouldn't apologize, because it is not my place to apologize for someone else, but I would explain that Ruth's passion for women's rights got the better of her for a moment. I would have a conversation with Isaac about the same articles I showed Ruth, and I would help him acknowledge that there are indeed women for whom a hijab is not a choice. Hopefully, after our conversation Isaac would be less aggrieved and would be able to accept Ruth's apology if it were forthcoming. But even if that were not so, he would have more of an understanding of where Ruth was coming from and would not feel so negatively toward her.

In all my interactions, I try very hard not to say something about any individual that I wouldn't say to their face. Obviously, this isn't always possible, but the aspiration has served me well.

This doesn't sound very "autistic," you may say. This way of thinking is probably inherent to any good mediator, although they may couch it using a different vocabulary.

Ah, but the vocabulary is so important here. It is precisely because I am committed to truth, the truest truth, the most brilliant facet of the truth, that I would have navigated the situation in the way I proposed.

I will never tell people what I think they want to hear. I truly don't know what they want to hear because I don't process body language well, or even verbal feedback, for that matter—at least not in the moment. Instead, I present my interlocutors with a brilliant facet of the truth, and it shines with a gentle light.

iii

The greatest truth-tellers (and the greatest liars) are small children, and I love spending time with them. I have four small boys of my own, and I wish I had a little girl. In another life I would have been a preschool teacher, listening to little piping voices all day and having delightful arguments with them over whether gummy bears were fruits. I don't get social headaches when I am with little children; I live in the moment with them and that relaxes me.

Part of my job as a congregational rabbi is running a Sunday school. This is probably the part of my job I am least suited to do. I don't like running things, and with a small Sunday school there are so many things that must be attended to on the fly: You have to be ready to substitute for the fourth-grade class because the teacher just tested positive for COVID-19, and you don't have a lesson plan, and your wife is home with a fever, so she can't help you with three of your restive children, who hang on to their father's leg while he is pontificating. You have to mollify parents who heard that a teacher mentioned God's name in class, which for some secular parents is worse than cussing, and you have to beg teachers to come to school despite having a sick relative at home. None of this is my forte. And yet, I get to interact with kids for two hours, and not just my own beautiful snot-faced progeny, but the children of others.

After every Sunday school session, I come home and hibernate in my room, hugging myself, and stimming because it was so hard. But it's worth it.

I have theories as to why I am good with little kiddos.

I think many of them intuitively observe that my manner lacks pretense, that I am guileless and take them at face value. As kids grow older and become more acculturated to fakey norms, I am less and less able to interact with them on this level; many have gone somewhere I can't follow. And yet even twelve-year-olds are still kids, and I love to see the freshness they bring to any topic. It is harder, but totally worth the effort.

Each Sunday before classes begin, all of the kids and parents meet together for a community circle. We discuss the holidays that are coming up, we sing songs, and we check in. A couple of years ago, at the beginning of the school year, I asked the assembled kids about the new foods they enjoyed eating during the fall festivals. I love talking and writing about food. A few kids mentioned berries and apples, and I mentioned blueberries (obviously). Then one ten-year-old mentioned that his favorite food was pig. He said this with a huge smile on his face. At first I thought that he was joshing me—I am a rabbi, after all, and perhaps I symbolized adherence to kosher culinary norms, which would have been somewhat ironic for the secular Jewish community I lead. But no, his father was Okinawan, and this boy loved pig. It was so wonderful that this kid felt comfortable enough to talk of his preference for the porcine in a Jewish Sunday school, where there were an above-average number of vegans. The honesty of children is so beautiful to behold. It reminds me of my own relationship with truth.

Another time, I was subbing for the seventh-grade teacher, and the topic was the hilarious holiday of Purim, whose most noteworthy traditions include a celebration of drunkenness and gender-bending costumes. There is also candy, of course. I had them take inventory of the leftover prizes and goodie bags from the year before, including a two-year-old bag of small chocolates at the bottom of the bin, which they pounced on like vultures upon a deer carcass, an apt metaphor considering the nutritional value of said chocolate. I never try to control seventh graders—they will do what they will, for their hormones rage—but I did try to reason with them. Abstract reasoning actually works with preteens, according to Piaget. Sometimes. I asked them to consider the age of the chocolate, and that their parents would treat me like that carcass I alluded to above if they consumed it on my watch. In the end I gave them agency, and most of them decided against taking the candy. No parent has called me yet to complain, so I guess I am in the clear. It is such a pleasure to watch kids make decisions informed by both logic and compassion. I am pretty sure I would have come to the same decision if I were twelve. But only pretty sure. Candy is candy, after all.

During the first COVID school year, our Sunday school met in Central Park. I love Central Park, and I love the *idea* of outdoor schooling. But Central Park is not an empty place, even in early December, and Sunday school classes are sadly not focused on nature as a primary theme. The teachers were absolute champs, and they used every trick in the book, and some in no book I know of, to keep the children focused and engaged. Our third-grade class tried to build the walls of Jericho out of the sticks in the clearing, but they kept falling down (the kiddos did not seem to mind). The high point for me was in December 2020: It was 38 degrees outside and we were celebrating Hanukkah. To keep warm, I pretended we were human dreidels and the person who could remain spinning longest without pause would win. My autistic son, Elisha, loved this and easily bested everyone. He'd probably still be there spinning if we hadn't needed to go home.

The fourth-grade teacher later told me what an unbelievably challenging year it had been. But she said that when she asked the kids whether they had had a good time, they told her the truth: They all had. For a dedicated teacher, that is all that counts.

iv

When I speak of truth, there is one poem I think about most. I wrote this at one of the hardest times of my life. In 2019, Aviva and I were expecting twins, which was a daunting but joyous prospect. Then three days before my wife's 36th birthday—a very symbolic birthday for many Jews, double chai, double life—we found out that one of our fetus' heartbeats had ceased. The girl I had always hoped for was dead.

Sometimes life breaks you.

I took my two-year-old home from school early that day and spent an hour hugging my sweet articulate tomato.

A few days later we found out that my close friend had also miscarried.

Our other fetus was tiny but thriving. But his was a very high-risk pregnancy. Medical literature gave him about a 25 percent chance of survival.

What followed were three and a half months of absolute hell. In the midst of the hell, I was supposed to function as a pastor of a congregation. I had only been seven months on the job at that point.

What was I to do?

I shared.

Miscarriage is such a common tragedy; so many families have experienced it. A family member of mine miscarried five times, and it hurts like hell. Like my friend who lost a baby at 27 weeks said, it is a club you never want to join, but after you have, everyone is kind to you. Because it is so common, people could relate to it, and we could have honest and hard conversations about how to cope with heartbreak.

And then there was the poem I wrote, the poem that encapsulated the excruciating time between the news that my daughter was dead and the emergency C-section that saved my son's life. This is my deepest truth.

What is hope?

Hope is hearing your baby's heartbeat
After his twin vanished
I want to call him a baby
not a fetus.

Hope is hearing that your child is not mentally retarded
He is just selectively mute
And one day he will choose to talk
And I will hear him

Hope is hearing your child pray
to a god you don't believe in
And breaking your heart
with the sweetness of his voice

And what, my love, is a broken heart?
It is the piercing of your reservoir of tears
By this dagger of hope
So that you can finally cry

Having difficult conversations is a critical part of community-building, and one that I have found I can do really well. The reason is that I cannot pretend to be something or someone I am not. I am by nature an oversharer.

This is my gift of truth.

Gift of Difference

One of the most critical jobs of a pastor or a rabbi is to create community from many individuals. This often leads us to speak of what binds us together, the values we share, the stories we share, and our cultural backgrounds.

But no less critical is to teach tolerance and embrace difference. Different family structures, different gender and sexual orientations, different races, and different neural make-ups.

I am different. I have always felt different, felt that something was off, that I didn't belong. I only found the words for that difference when I was an adult.

The current estimate of those on the autism spectrum is about two percent. That is probably an underestimate, considering the success of those on the high-functioning band of the spectrum at masking their more noticeable autistic behaviors. I am one of those "successes."

I can present myself as neurotypical so well that only my most discerning interlocutors can tell that this is not the case.

Throughout my life, I have deliberately worked on eliminating many of those autistic behaviors. I was doing this way before I discovered language for my difference. I gaze back at my childhood and early adulthood and it makes me sad and angry at the world that I had to work so hard to change my neural wiring.

When I was kid, I never looked people in the eye. It caused me physical discomfort, something between a scratch and a sprain. It still does, but less so, and I still have to tell myself every day, "Look people in the eye, otherwise they will think you are weird."

All my life I have stimmed. Stimming is a comforting patterned movement. I used to wave my arms around wildly; now I shake my legs side to side or up and down when sitting. People still notice it sometimes, but less often. I wish I could still stim like I used to. My beautiful little boy stands on his head on the sofa to comfort himself—the only time I stop him is if he is eating Cheerios and could choke.

I've adapted, but I will never think that it's fair. None of my behaviors harmed anyone.

The above paragraphs are an attenuated version of the rants of my twenties, which included many expletives to indicate how angry I actually was.

My therapist would likely tell me it's also a sign of classical masking, if truth be told, with perhaps a tinge of perfectly normal passive-aggressiveness.

One of the most important lessons of my thirties was to learn to laugh at myself instead of cry and exert more control over my anger—to sublimate it and channel it.

These days, I don't take myself very seriously. I guess I probably could if I wanted to. I am a morbidly over-credentialed human specimen. The temptation to take myself too seriously is eternally there—the sweet fruit on the tree of ego. After all, why did I spend all that time acquiring accolades if not to be taken seriously by others?

But whenever I am tempted to, I think of the many times I made a fool of myself, take a deep breath, and go eat some walnut date ice cream. I think of the time when I vomited on Zoom while teaching a class. I could have moved away from the camera; instead, I moved toward it. A couple of people left the class and never came back. I think of the time I was practicing a throw in karate, and instead of kicking someone's legs from under them, I kicked myself where the sun rarely shines. I think of the many, many times I made a fool of myself in pursuit of women until I met someone who didn't mind that.

If we are honest with ourselves, we must admit that we are all foolish sometimes. That is part of being human. If we learn to laugh at our mistakes, it will be easier to move on and improve—at least until the next time we slip on a banana peel. Which leads me to the question: I am different, but so what? So is someone with ADHD. So is someone in a wheelchair. So is someone with darker skin.

What kind of accommodation am I asking from society?

I am asking for *no* accommodation from society on my behalf. I have worked like the dickens to accommodate myself. And now I can ruefully laugh at the path I have taken, at the mistakes along the way.

The path was hard, and it did not need to be as hard, which is why I am asking—no, that is not accurate—I am demanding accommodation on behalf of any person who cannot for whatever reason advocate effectively enough for themselves, whose voices are not resonating, because the deck is so stacked against them.

People like my son Elisha, who is presently on a deeper band of the autism spectrum, who may never be able to articulate his needs.

I know it is so friggin' difficult to live with significant difference, and that is why I make it a cornerstone of my mission to create a space for difference in my community.

This is the gift of difference.

The Gift of Poetry

How can you be both poetic and literal? I am.

And I can tell you why this is not a contradiction.

The opposite of literal is figurative or fictional. An example of this is the "love" button on Twitter. Believe me, I don't actually love most of the statements I Twitter-love; I only vaguely approve of the fuzzy kitten picture my passing acquaintance posted. (I am not really a cat person.) "Love" is used representationally as approval. This bothers me deeply, and I still feel like I am a fraud when I apply pressure to a button on my keyboard to "love" something, but I have managed to somehow rationalize it. You may think I am exaggerating my discomfort here. I am not. Believe me when I tell you, literalness is hardwired into my brain.

Poetry is full of images and representations, wordplay and flowery alliteration, so when I write that "the kiss of my lover rises upwards and creates the world," I am not being literal. My kiss is a physical act and has no corporeality enabling it to rise, no wings that allow it to fly, let alone physically create. I am employing several figures of speech when I do this.

But unlike the execrable "love" button of Twitter, in poetry I aspire to a deeper truth. When I was writing about this kiss, I was writing about the first kiss I enjoyed with my lover and now wife. That kiss created something entirely new in me, something that I had not experienced ever before, and that was love.

And that is in essence what I try to do when I write poetry. I try to find language for the deeper truths of my experience, and sometimes for the experience of others.

Poetry is at the very core of who I am.

ii

My life has been a search for the words that would express who I was.

The beginnings were pathetic.

Like many on a certain band of the autism spectrum, I was very gifted with language acquisition and read four languages when I was six, but this was entirely a passive act. As a kid, I did not advance much beyond my childhood poetry of: "Your name is *caca masara*, you are a bad boy," the height of my prowess in first-grade. I was a C- student in English up till ninth-grade, and that is not because the teacher didn't like me because I was autistic. (Though she didn't.)

It was because I had not figured out how to use words to any real effect. And also, being told you suck at something day in and day out doesn't often lead to good outcomes.

And then something clicked. I'd just left my private Jewish high school in Toronto and was in transition to the hellish boarding school my parents had inflicted upon me. To make matters extra special, they sent me to summer school so I could keep up my English. The teenage years are so full of unfairness. My progenitors' problematic parenting choices catalyzed a devil-may-care attitude in me that summer. I had been told by many people that my talents, as they were, lay elsewhere—such as retreading tires—ever since I was given a time out in kindergarten for writing an S backwards. Something just broke loose, and I really wrote for the very first time. I wrote with my angry heart. I got the second-highest grade in the class, and would have gotten the highest had I cared about coming to class remotely on time. The vocabulary from reading a book a day since I'd been six had finally filtered through. I never got less than an A in any class that involved creative composition from that point until I handed in my PhD eight and a half years later.

Yet, despite my burgeoning skills with the qwerty keyboard, I still lacked the words to express the fundamental questions: "Who am I?" and "why don't I get it?"

There is a wonderful story about identity that I loved as a child: The story of the mysterious Aussie bogeymonster the bunyip, written by Jennifer Wagner. It starts with a mysterious creature poking his head out of the mud of Berkeley's Creek. The creature does not know what he is until a passing wallaby tells him, you are a bunyip. The bunyip is initially content with this knowledge but then becomes dissatisfied, for he does not know what he looks like. The bunyip keeps asking creatures of the Australian outback about himself. They all say he and his features are the height of ugliness. He is sad but still hopeful. During his wanderings he meets a man; after examining him, the man tells him that bunyips "simply don't exist." Deflated, the bunyip goes to a comfortable billabong and decides to be alone. He is happy in his aloneness, or at the very least content. But that night, for no particular reason, another creature pops out of the mud of the billabong. She asks, "Who am I?" and ecstatic, he answers, "You are a bunyip."

I was a bunyip without words to describe myself until I was 28.

iii

But first, a few more stations on my writing journey.

At the first of these stations, when I was 19, I learned a valuable lesson about regurgitation.

In academia, at least as an undergrad, you are expected to regurgitate the knowledge of the ages, not try to write something interesting or original with your piddling skills. When I realized this, my grades rose from a B to an A+. This is a big part of the reason why students at so many institutions marinate for years in grad school without being able to write anything interesting or original.

I am someone who has been deeply blessed with creativity because of the neural wiring bequeathed to me by genetics. But I do believe that creativity can be taught and that regurgitation is not the way to go about it. Regurgitation leads to calcification of neural pathways and to series of books on biblical prepositions.

I am forever indebted to Hebrew University for teaching me critical thinking and skepticism, and yes, saying it like it is without hiding behind religious dogma. My questions about the Bible were answered, but my questions about who I was remained unanswered.

When I was 24, I was inducted into the Israeli army. I guess if I were an idealogue of any sort, I would have either enjoyed it, or left the country, or gone to jail to prevent it. But I was not and am not, and since I was a male Jewish citizen of Israel, I was legally obligated to serve. So I did.

My initial model for military service was Forrest Gump, who follows orders without thinking about them and is told he will be a general someday. I was one of the three soldiers in my battalion of inductees to get cited for distinction, which was pretty remarkable since at the shooting range, I only managed three out of ten.

I got placed in the IDF's history department because of my academic background. Great for my own development, not necessarily a good use of manpower by the military.

You see, since I was a small child, I've had two conflicting forces at war in my psyche. The first was a deep respect for order, which meant following rules. And the second was a commitment to sing in my own off-key voice. My first-grade teacher, the only teacher I ever loved in any school system, said, "Tzemah knows his own mind, and does not bow to peer pressure." This meant that if an injustice was perpetrated, I would speak up no matter the repercussions to me, and if a rule did not make sense, I would not follow it. The second of these tendencies does not work well in the military.

But not following rules in the army gets you sent to the slammer, and I knew that, so I followed them to my own offbeat tune. I was in charge of translating military drivel from English into Hebrew and vice versa, but I translated only four pages a day (that seemed to be enough to satisfy the powers that be), which took me a couple of hours. The rest of the time I dreamed, and I wrote.

I learned a lot about asymmetric warfare and about Israel's early years. I brought my finely honed BS detector, and I became an angry cynic. I learned the facts behind Israel's wars, and I unlearned the propagandistic version of history I had been taught in my Jewish schools. I vacillated between left-wing Zionism and post-Zionism, and I learned how to write the most beautiful expletive-laced rants.

I started to apply this skepticism to every part of my life—to my sexual orientation, to my religious praxis, to every part of my identity—and I flirted with nihilism. Most specifically, I questioned the language of the prayers I had been saying since I was a toddler and observed that I believed nothing of them whatsoever.

iv

I thankfully don't know what would have been the end result of this downward spiral—perhaps I would have ended up a smear on the pavement somewhere, because it was at that time I was given advice that changed the course of my life. I was studying rabbinics at some unknown non-academic institution for the lack of anything better to do after the army and zero job prospects. I asked the head of the institution if I could be exempted from daily prayer because I felt entirely like a fraud. And then he told me: If you don't believe in what you're saying, compose your own liturgy. And I did.

So instead of nihilism, I created something. I created a liturgy that expressed my deeply held beliefs about the world and my place in it, and it was beautiful.

I had my words.

I had the matches, and I had the wood, but Prometheus had not yet given me fire.

And then it happened.

When I was 28, I read a book. I read a memoir which turned me inside out: I discovered a second bunyip, and he gave a name to my neurodivergence. I was a high-functioning autistic person, but I will forever prefer the dated and problematic term Asperger's, because that is the first word I had to describe myself.

Excited, I told my parents about my discovery. After reading about autistic people for fifteen minutes, my father told me I did not exist. He did not believe me. And so I hid my identity from everyone except my diary. Here is what I wrote that day sixteen years ago. The anger is entirely raw. In my diary I name it "The Discovery."

The Discovery

"The other day I found out why I was so f-ed up as a kid. The name of the game was Asperger's. Asperger's is not a genus of vegetable, nor is it the name of a cute kitten. It is a disorder, identified in the past ten years, the symptoms of which are social antipathy, an inability to tell right from left, and a tendency to shit your pants because of an allergy to wheat. Thankfully, there is an upside to all this crap: Many sufferers have enhanced linguistic and mathematical aptitude, euphemistically referred to as idiot savant abilities, but since we are so f-ed up we usually don't have any good way to apply these gifts. I discovered my Aspergerity after reading Daniel Tammet's autobiography. Daniel Tammet holds the world record in the recital of pi, 22,514 (give or take), and can learn how to speak a language in a week. I finished my doctorate in Bible when I was 24, and I can learn how to read a language in two weeks. How has this discovery affected me, you may ask? Well, for one thing, I can now yell at my parents for all the shit they dumped on me as a kid for just not getting it (actually, they didn't) and avoid responsibility for everything I've screwed up at throughout my life. That seems like the healthy and mature way to deal with my problems.

Asperger's is optimistically referred to as high-functioning autism. I think I buy two out of three words in that definition. I am definitely autistic, and I am high much of the time on ego's sweet delusions. To say that I am functioning is optimistic."

None of what my 28-year-old self said is remotely politically correct or factually accurate, but the rage at the world is so raw. My wife, who met me a year later, remembers my world-famous rants. That she married me in spite of this is a testament to the statement by Forrest Gump that miracles can happen.

I never saw myself as having a disability, even though autism is sometimes classified as such. I was just me. Perhaps acknowledging my difficulty to others and speaking about my experiences would have helped me on the job market and on the flesh market. I know I botched several interviews because of body language, inappropriate tone, dressing incorrectly, etc. And I excruciatingly f-d up innumerable interactions with women for similar reasons.

But I eventually saw Asperger's as a blessing as well. A blessing that gave me an exceptionally good memory, gave me a gift of language and numbers, and the spark of creativity. I just had to find where to light it.

V

Sit back, my friend, and you shall hear of a truly unlikely career. I got canned like tuna in 2009 when the unctuous unworthies who hired me for a tenure-track job decided they couldn't afford to pay me minimum wage but could afford three deans for 40 students. In other words, the usual. The dammit of course was that I had left Israel for La La Land, and it was a bit hard to go back to the guns and the insane politics. So instead, my spouse started grad school, and we lived like frugal rabbits for a while.

For the past five or six years, I'd been rewriting Jewish liturgy to conform to my idiosyncratic theology, which had garnered me some negative press but no big bucks. It did get me into rabbinical school, though, and I thought that doing that was at least marginally better than playing video games. Rabbinical school is often a path to a rewarding career, if you are an Orthodox, Conservative, or Reform rabbi. It is not if you are an atheist. I am the type of guy who organized religion burned at the stake until quite recently. So I did not expect this to go anywhere.

I also wrote popular-sounding books about the Bible like *The First Book of God* and *God Didn't Write the Bible*, but my sales aspired to awfulness. Usually my audience was me, myself, and my psychiatrist. Your dad may have taught you that if you persevere at something for long enough, you will become marginally better at it. I became quite good at this type of writing.

So for a while I just wrote, changed diapers, and stewed in my own juices. My wife worked her butt off and climbed the rungs of her career, so we could generally pay the rent. But I also wanted to perpetuate my genes, and after child number three we decided we couldn't afford both my blueberry habit and housing. Well, she decided, and threatened me with divorce. I gave in and started looking. The problem was I was stuck in the same rut I described above. I may have finished two PhDs, but I absolutely abhorred the debasement of the academic job application, and I hadn't written many academic articles.

The only places for me to apply were thus community colleges and the adjunct circuit, so probably not worth the investment of time. But having two documents attesting to my advanced knowledge of esoteric ancient texts written in Hebrew and Septuagint Greek is not as worthless as you may think. They were a sign that I was likely in the third or fourth standard deviation north of a normal IQ, and so could actually think.

I also possessed an idiosyncratic rabbinical degree from atheists anonymous, which I considered a curiosity. But, to my great surprise, in the United Estates of America, where separation of church and state is celebrated, that actually tipped the balance.

vi

I introduced myself to City Congregation with a talk about Jewish love poetry.

I shared all my gifts in that moment.

My songs of love were in eight different languages, for I possess the gift of tongues, and I was in the heart of multicultural New York.

I spoke truthfully about my experiences in the emergency room with my infant son, and how I sang the very simplest love song I knew to a tiny being who I could not touch.

I unpacked the songs and poems for my audience, transforming the figurative into literal truths so those who do not like poetry, or who are unaccustomed to it, could understand what I was trying to say in these poems.

Without pretense or guile, I sang the songs that I knew in my gravelly off-tune voice, and led by imperfect example.

When people asked me quasi-invasive questions about my background, about who I was, I spoke honestly about being different. I spoke about being on the spectrum, about being married to an Orthodox-ordained rabbi, about being Israeli. I hid very little. For I cannot hide.

And I read my own poems, inviting people to know me deeply and truly.

I spoke about the universal patterns one could find in these love songs, from the most ancient to the most modern, hoping that I would strike a chord and they would hire me. And they did.

My talk, revised for this occasion, can be found at the back of this book. If you are so inclined, I invite you to follow me to the banks of the river on Sabbath's eve and read this overture to my congregation.

The Gift of Aloneness

I love to be alone in front of a computer, munching blueberries and writing poems.

Okay, it doesn't have to be blueberries, but at the very least it should be a round food, mildly sweet and bought at a farmer's market.

I want to do this, or activities that resemble this, most of my life.

I want to be left alone. A lot of the time.

So why in the hell did I join the rabbinate and consent to answer prying questions like what is the meaning of life? Why did you say this in the sermon? Are you an atheist or are you a fake?

Kind of acerbic, but entirely valid.

I could have become a number cruncher at some science institute. After all, my autism spectrum gifts include mathematical aptitude. I probably could have earned a boatload more money doing this. So why indeed?

One of the most enduring misconceptions about people on the spectrum, at least my particular band of the spectrum, is our relationship to others.

When I was in my late twenties, I was very lucky to be in a social group that accepted me for who I was (for the most part). I could come over for a Friday night dinner and then go up to the loft and read a fantasy book by Guy Gavriel Kay, and then join them afterwards for wine and singing. I loved that. I even had a way of drinking wine named after me. To do a Tzemah was to fill a large drinking glass, specifically not a wineglass, and chug.

I accept the necessity of others. I more than accept it—I crave company, just on different terms than my neurotypical brethren.

I need to be alone a lot, but I want the comforting presence of others, who acknowledge that I am a worthwhile human being, in the background. I need others. Others are like beautiful classical music when you are on the Henry Hudson in New York and Google Maps has just announced an hour delay and informed you that you are on the fastest route.

Eating blueberries and writing poetry is not a viable career path. And in truth I wouldn't want it to be.

I am not a classic introvert. I do want to have meaningful interactions with others. I have four little boys and a spouse I love to bits. I actually derive intense pleasure from being with people.

It is true that introversion is sometimes a good first step to understanding my band on the autism spectrum. Before I acquired the language of autism, I could self-classify as an introvert, and that definitely helped. People get introversion. People understand social headaches and feeling drained by having to interact with others for lengthy periods of time. But I am an autistic person, not an introvert or not just an introvert. The intensity of my headaches is not because I am inherently drained by social interaction, or because of some misanthropic tendencies. It is because I am trying so hard to understand the situation I am in, and because of my neural wiring, this understanding is not inherent or intuitive. It requires more of me than it would of someone neurotypical. And often I want to take this extra effort because other human beings are wonderful.

My poor brain goes into overdrive, but not because I am trying to impress anyone; I am just trying to stay afloat. I am expending calories like an Olympic distance runner, but instead of sweating the calories out from all the pores of my body, my CPU/head overheats, and then I get a headache.

Like the Olympic distance runner, I love what I do. I love interacting with others. It is just that I need breaks frequently. I need to be alone.

Being the rabbi of a small congregation is not a full-time job. I have time for my blueberries and my writing. Writing meaningful liturgy and sermons is actually an important part of my job, and I enjoy it so much. And when it is necessary, I can be fully present for people. This is usually a good balance.

This recognition of my need for balance, and my ability to fashion my life so that I am able to live it out, is a gift, a gift of my hard-earned self-awareness.

A fellow journeyer on a similar band of the spectrum once tweeted that autistic people are often seen as uncompassionate and cold. We are not. Not as a group. In his description, "We are so compassionate, it hurts."

The Gift of Being Literal

Being literal, and then trying to compensate for it, creates a cognitive dissonance that makes life interesting and sometimes funny.

It makes certain spicy pejoratives interesting to contemplate, even though I know I shouldn't take them literally.

When I was a kid, though, I had not yet developed that cognitive sophistication, and I always, always took things at face value.

When I was six, I took an IQ test. I did not do well.

Not "he needs to go to a special place" badly, but bad enough that private schools looked at my parents in bemusement when they tried to enroll me.

I was dull.

I don't remember very much from this test, except for two questions:

I was asked to find the shortest path through a maze. I did. I drew a straight line from point A to point B.

The examiner tried to keep his demeanor steady and said, no, no, young man, you cannot touch any lines.

So I drew another straight line, and this time, whenever I got to a border of the maze, my pencil jumped.

I thought to myself, give me another easy one!

Another question was who discovered America. Now the answer you are expected to give is of a certain Spanish dude who sailed in 1492.

I promise you I knew that when I was six.

But please note that the question was not which European discovered America, it was more general. And so I said tribes that had crossed the Bering Strait thirty thousand years ago. Another grand slam, I thought.

It wasn't that I was precociously woke when I was six. My liberal academic parents had simply bought me a child's encyclopedia and I had read through it.

Needless to say, my answers did not impress the examiner.

It took me many years to learn to give the answers others expect, rather than the truth, on standardized tests. Now I score in the top percentile. But whenever I have the misfortune of being examined, it still gives me a very bad itch to mark something right even when I know with all my heart and soul it is not. But I do it.

As an adult I have learned to translate my gift of literalness into a capacity to take people at face value. When someone tells me something about themselves, I believe it.

Does that make me naïve?

Maybe. I know that people lie, but I cannot recognize falsehood easily. So I almost always give people the benefit of the doubt. I try to see people the way they wish to be seen. When I encounter a situation, I attribute benevolent and worthy motivations to actions.

I believe that when you see people as they wish to be seen, when you see people in the best possible light, you elevate them. And even if they have lied to you, even if they have misrepresented themselves, there is potential for their lies to become truth. There is potential for them to become better people.

ii

My literalness profoundly informs my belief system. As someone who cannot easily intuit what others are thinking and feeling, I tend to rely on the observable, what I literally see. I have not observed any reason to assume a benevolent deity governing the world, and thus I vacillate between agnosticism and atheism. A fair number of studies have linked autism spectrum disorder with atheistic tendencies—and I buy that. We cannot easily understand other minds, so it would be a real stretch to imagine the greatest Otherness imaginable—such a notion would be entirely foreign and strange.

I am thus a wonderful ideological fit with secular humanists who want to govern their lives without recourse to supernatural authority. Ever since I came into my own as a teenager and stopped fearing the bogeyman God—who would kill me if I didn't say sorry on the Day of Atonement or if I had an errant sexual thought—I have been what is euphemistically referred to as a freethinker.

In other ways, I am not such a good fit. I am a very traditional person. I observe many of the Sabbath customs, and my household is kosher. I celebrate all the holidays, even the minor ones, and fast on Yom Kippur and Tisha B'Av. I even recite liturgy on a daily basis, though not to God, of course. I am married to a woman who was ordained by Orthodox rabbis, and that naturally impacts how I live my life as well.

A key difference between me and an Orthodox person, though, is that I am quite mindful about the reasons I do things. I am very deliberate. If a tradition does not make sense to me, or is ethically problematic in any way, I simply will not observe it. If a blessing does not ring true to me, I will not recite it. I cannot suspend disbelief for more than a couple of minutes.

Some people would call this religious humanism and then leave my congregation, as some indeed have. In a way, they would be right, but in a different and more fundamental way they would be wrong. My way of thinking is entirely secular: My humanism is my ethical compass, and the Torah and rabbinic law are simply parts of my cultural heritage and in no way authoritative.

A number of years ago I was visiting Okinawa, Japan, to pay homage to the head of my martial arts style. My hosts, two very high-ranking black belts, barely understood a word of English, but generously showed me around the island. It was a very rewarding experience. My last evening on the island, they took me out to dinner at a gourmet restaurant: McDonald's. True fact—in some countries in the Far East, American fast food is considered to be an exotic delicacy, just as we may enjoy French cuisine. This is quite difficult for me to wrap my head around, considering that my opinion of McDonald's and its ilk gravitates between nauseating and merely disgusting. Yet there they took me. I had no way of communicating with them that McDonald's was not appetizing or kosher, indeed, that it epitomized non-Kosherness for North American Jews like nothing else. They did not know about Jews or about their dietary practices. I did not want to insult my hosts, who had treated me so nicely, so I ate a whole order of Chicken McNuggets with extra fries. It was clear to me that had I refused to eat with them, it would have hurt their feelings and damaged our relationship. Since I do not feel bound or commanded to keep the laws of kashrut, but rather view them as a valued tradition, I chose to follow the guiding principle of humanist philosophy—treat others the way you yourself would like to be treated—rather than kashrut. It was just too bad that I had to eat Chicken McNuggets to prove it instead of Lobster a La King.

iii

A Jewish value that I believe in wholeheartedly is being there for people during the most important moments of their lives. At naming ceremonies, at weddings, and yes, also at funerals.

One traditional Jewish prayer states:

> *These are the things the value of which is immeasurable.... They are repaid in this world and the balance appreciates in the world to come: welcoming guests, visiting the sick, bringing in the bride and the groom, and accompanying the dead... and bringing peace between a person and their fellow.*

I don't buy into the supernatural paradigm, or accept that there is a world to come, of course, but I do believe in the value of acting in this way.

Not all of these occasions are equal.

Welcoming guests, attending weddings—these are intrinsically satisfying. You often feel good in the moment, a veritable win-win situation. Well, this might not be true if you are introverted and autistic, but for many.

When you attend a funeral, and especially if you officiate at one, you often end up feeling depleted. There is no happiness in the room. People are not inclined to thank you. You are constantly being judged by the attendees. The deep irony for me is that I shine at funerals. I hate them, but I shine.

I have had the misfortune of officiating only at funerals of people I did not know well or at all. So, it was always very hard to relate to the person as a full human being. Maybe that is fortunate in a selfish way. I have not officiated at the funeral of someone I love.

Before a funeral, I make sure to talk to the closest friends and family members of the deceased to learn about their loved one. I have no way to judge the truth of what they tell me. I just absorb it and ask questions. I take what I hear at face value. Literally.

I have learned that people tell me mostly the good parts. I am sure there are bad parts, but I don't hear them. Hear no evil, see no evil, is a good way to approach funerals.

And then I bring a piece of poetry. I always bring poetry into it.

At one funeral I heard from a friend of the dead person that her favorite flower was lilacs. And so I quoted snippets of a poem by Walt Whitman on lilacs, which inspired many of the eulogizers to also quote poetry—poetry that the deceased had written but never published. I found out that one of her favorite songs was "You Are My Sunshine," which changes so radically when you know the verses instead of just the chorus. I sang it with my very imperfect voice and the audience joined in, and then some people who actually know how to sing were inspired.

Poetry is a perfect vehicle to capture complexity on these occasions, to say what cannot be said directly. To speak about the sadness of this person's death and what they left behind.

Sometimes I google the deceased. I do live in the 21st century, after all, and I know how to use technology. Once I found an article the deceased had written in the '70s for the *New York Times*, an article demonstrating his deep compassion, and I quoted from it.

Some of this would have happened without me, but I have been at funerals that were absolutely horrible experiences, so I think it is okay to take some credit as an officiant when things go well.

I was one of the eulogizers at my grandfather's funeral. My grandfather survived Auschwitz and was rescued by the Russian army. He ate a horse. He almost lost a leg. One of the moments he shone most was when he had the opportunity to kill a Nazi soldier and did not. He spared him.

The rabbi officiating got that tiny detail wrong. He said that my grandfather had killed the guy. OMG, and this rabbi had literally known my grandfather for fifty years. Everything else the schmo said was lost on me. Doing funerals well matters. It matters profoundly. If you get it wrong, the moment is marked indelibly in the memory of the attendees forever.

It always seemed to me that I was a big disappointment to my grandfather. Such good grades. Such potential. But I didn't go into business, law, or medicine, ostensibly the only acceptable professions in his eyes. Scratch that. I am not sure professions mattered, financial success mattered. I think my grandfather would have been fine with me had I had 10 million dollars in my bank account no matter what I did.

The last words I heard him say, after making an off-color joke about the 'ganefs' [thieves] in Transylvania, were about my employment. At the time of my grandfather's death I was still deep in my freelance writing phase and supporting my wife by taking care of my beautiful son most of the day. My grandfather was of a different generation; he didn't understand this. A man must support his family financially, otherwise what is he worth? My last memory of my grandfather is his slight smile of what I interpreted as disappointment. I hope it wasn't.

The man had supported me through college. He'd bought me my first apartment. I owed him so much. And now one of my main associations with him will be the officiating rabbi calling him a murderer! It is so important to do funerals well.

I hope I do not have to officiate at a congregant's funeral anytime soon, but when it does happen, I'll know what to do. I will listen, I will try to find a fitting poem, and I will tell you all the ways this person shone in the world from the perspective of those who loved them. I will present the literal, most brilliant facet of truth.

Gift of Patterns / Gift of Veils

One of my favorite pieces of biblical literature is Ecclesiastes 3, immortalized in English by the beautiful rendition of the Byrds:

> To everything there is a season
> and a time to every purpose under heaven.
> A time to be born and a time to die,
> A time to cast away stones
> and a time to gather stones together.

This appeals to me fundamentally.

I am autistic and I live a very patterned life. I enjoy my daily routines, which ground me. At 5:15 a.m. I wake up, and I spend the first 45 minutes reading about 10 articles in various online presses. At 6, my son Nadav gets up—he wants to be with his mother, and I transport him there. I then work on translating or writing a new book for about 15 minutes. And then I do some poetry.

Anything out of the ordinary is a stress factor. A difficulty.

Stress is not inherently a bad thing! It is not a four-letter word; it is six letters long.

Stress becomes a deliberate catalyst to try something new. I incorporate stress into the pattern of my days. I plan for the inevitability of stress.

If my son Jaime starts screaming like a banshee at 3:30 a.m., either because of a bogeyman or because he wants candy, obviously my morning is not going to look the same; I am not going to get the same things done. That is difficult. But like an experienced surfer, I ride the wave of exhaustion and do something with it. I write a poem about quality time at 3 a.m. with my lovely four-year-old. I can't translate, I can't do emails, but I have found, like other people who write, that particular flavors of exhaustion are conducive to creativity.

Even on bad nights, there is generally an hour or two of lucidity in the mornings when I can get important emails done, such as explaining to the board in excruciating detail why a kids' service is not desirable for a particular event, so I do manage to work.

And then at noon, when the little imps are resting, I can lay down my tired head and sleep.

Exhaustion and stressors simply lead to a different type of pattern, which I fall into after figuring out the nature of the situation.

That is why I can live in the world COVID-19 has fashioned. I am genuinely embarrassed to say that I have actually thrived during these past few years in ways I never thought possible.

Because in a fundamental way, the COVID-19 world is *my* world. It allowed me the time and space to discover what was most important to me in my interactions with family, friends, peers, and colleagues.

For many years I have struggled with how exactly to define my deep need for others. The caricatured autistic person is someone who doesn't need anyone else, who lives in their own mind, who is an island deep in the ocean and untethered to land while the rest of the people of the world are at the very least peninsulas. This is of course bullshit, as I have articulated a few times. Autistic people need others, just in different ways than our neurotypical brethren. I often need the comforting presence of others near me while I do my own thing. I need my wife to sleep next to me, otherwise my sleep is disturbed. I need my two-year-old to call for Abba at 6 a.m. each morning so I can pick him up and kiss him, and then I need him to ignore me the rest of the morning because he wants to be with his mother. I need others to validate my existence, but I also need partial anonymity. I need a veil.

That is why the COVID world is my world. It has imposed a veil between so many of us. A veil no one has chosen, a veil of necessity. For so many people the veil has been destructive: Extroverts have been cut off from each other and have found the virtual world a pale shadow that cannot replace in-person interaction. A veritable plague of mental health problems has been the result of forced separation. The continuity and patterns some kids need to thrive in their educational frameworks has been cut off root and branch. And so on.

And then there are people like me, people who feel guilty for how they have survived and thrived. Suddenly the expectations and pressure surrounding face-to-face interactions have ceased. The need to look other people in the eye is gone—no one can tell anymore. And in public everyone is wearing a mask anyway, so they can't read people's expressions, just as I can't.

I have found that I can create so much more content for my congregation because I am less tired. I can teach more classes, make more phone calls, and be present. I could never do that as fully as I wanted to before the pandemic; it would have been too draining. There is much less forced small talk, which is so very hard for me. When there is conversation, a higher ratio of it is meaningful and substantive, and that is such a pleasure!

But at some point, it will be normal to congregate freely and safely. By that time, though, I will have figured out when the veil between me and the world should continue to exist, and when I should take it off to gaze upon the world.

Gift of Tongues

Like rose cardamom dark chocolate, with its perfect balance between sweetness and smoothness and taste, like flower petals on the tongue, sometimes my poems achieve transcendence. It doesn't happen often. But when it does—oh my.

There are so many traditional pieces of prayer I love. But I can't sing them. More accurately, I won't sing them, for I am an atheist and do not believe in any God you can conceive of. Nor am I able to suspend disbelief for a long enough span to comfortably sing traditional songs. I am on the spectrum, and I am literal. If I don't believe it, I can't say it.

As we say in Yiddish, this is a *shanda*. So many traditional prayers are appealing to my aesthetics, especially those that are Hebraically rich, in poetic meter, and yet linear and simple.

What do I do?

I shift the words. Sometimes that leads to some mild approbation from fellow poets, but usually it goes nowhere. Once it led to something so much bigger. Before I share how I came to sing one particular poem, and how it blew up my conception of what liturgy could do in cultural Jewish communities, perhaps I should share with you a bit more of an explanation of why I've written new liturgy for the past two decades. This is another snippet of my journey.

The words of a wise man catalyzed the font of poetry and prayer that has emerged through my fingertips and unto countless computer files. I never forget that. But it was and is something deep within me that compels me to write liturgy almost every day.

It's the dissonance at the very heart of my Jewish experience.

ii

I love the sound of Hebrew poetry, the wondrous aesthetics of mellifluous alliteration I can only find in the best crafted pieces of liturgical compositions. But! But the content is always, always wrong. It never says what I want it to say. It never expresses my truth.

In the beginning, I was very angry about this. This is how I expressed it in my diary when I was 28:

> *My first memory of the temples inculcating patriarchalism otherwise known as synagogues is my grandpappy's dear house of worship. There was a lot of mumbling going on by oldsters and my mother was cordoned up with a group of women in their best gossiping about how much money their neighbors didn't have. For me it was a toss-up—malicious gossip or mumbling golden agers who had sweet things in their pockets for lucky little boys. I chose to stay with my mother...*
>
> *My mother emphasized to me at an early age that there was no difference between boys and girls except for genitalia. So why did girls get to sit with their mommies and look pretty while we boys had to mutter, "God is one God is great"–in the words of recalcitrant Pharaoh, who was God and why for Pete's sake did I have to say those words? My mother told me that she and my father fought over who would get to take care of me and my baby bro—outside of the synagogue, where they couldn't*

hear their coreligionists chanting words they didn't know to a being they couldn't see.

I am less angry now, because I have shifted my world in the way I wanted to and I have words. But it does not mean I wasn't very alone. Here is how I expressed it more recently to a band of rabbis, when I spoke to them about the isolation inherent in being Hebraically literate:

> *Hebrew is my mother tongue. I speak in Hebrew to my children, I compose prayers in Hebrew, and both my dissertations focus on intensive philological analyses of ancient Hebrew texts. There is nothing I enjoy more than reading and sometimes singing ancient Hebrew with obsessive accuracy. And yet, the progressive bent of my North American Jewish affiliations precludes the full expression of this love because neither exactitude nor fluency in Hebrew are deeply valued in these environments. This is especially true of the humanist community I lead, where Torah is not read and Hebrew is secondary. This is entirely justified, considering the community values, and where they come from. But what about me?*
>
> *One of the profound contradictions in my life is that fluency and love for this type of Hebrew engagement is only found in right-wing communities, both religiously and politically. Sometimes I sneak into Orthodox synagogues and guiltily indulge in these cadences, but I have to sneak right back out lest I hear a sermon, which I may be seen as tacitly endorsing.*

I must apologize lest this sound elitist in any way. Mostly it brings me heartache and loneliness.

The lack of emphasis on rigorous Hebraic knowledge in the liberal Jewish communities of North America has always saddened me, but this sadness is a bit selfish. I don't actually think that a deep knowledge of Hebrew is necessary for a rewarding Jewish life in North America. There are just so many ways to be Jewish today, and a deep engagement with Hebrew compositions, while important, is only one avenue. Mainly, I am lonely and crave interlocutors. I want people to talk to about my progressive liturgical poetry informed by the piyyut tradition, and there is really no one with whom I can have a deeply informed conversation, who would challenge me and take my work to new places. Maybe I have not searched as much as I could have.

And yet there is a silver lining that affords me some comfort. My loneliness has pushed me to become a translator of my own compositions, and to write and explain in English, which I see as important, not just to me, but to the communities I inhabit. This has the corollary of forcing me to re-engage deeply with my liturgy on a regular basis, to find new ways to express my truths. In fact, I would say that most of my liturgical regimen these days involves this type of translating and editing. This is probably the aspect of rabbi-ing that I find most fulfilling. It is what propelled me to the rabbinate in the first place, and is really my primary

solace as a congregational leader who is always just a
bit discombobulated.

And though our lips are adept at offering approbation
At formulating pithy metaphors and mellifluous
alliteration
We cannot repay what we owe
With verbiage and show

My loneliness doesn't mean that I don't dream though, and my dream, my ideal, is singing rich liturgical compositions that reflect my values with a community that can appreciate them.

iii

Sometimes dreams come true. Last Day of Atonement, I was moved by liturgy in a way I never have been. I sang a poetically resonant piece of liturgy, which I had composed, and it was glorious. Here is how I processed it in the moment:

> On the Day of Atonement at about 4 p.m. in the afternoon, I have the same doubts that Bialik did when he said, "O heavens, ask for mercy on my behalf, if God is there, and there is a path to him, for I have not found it." Bialik's desperation refers to the complete apathy of God and extreme doubt, but at 4 p.m. I am more concerned with the glacial movement of the day toward its completion. How can I be moved by liturgy toward something greater when I am so ridiculously hungry!
>
> This may be the inescapable irony of the Day of Atonement, but I think Avraham Ben Yitzhak provides an answer. In a beautiful piece about the final prayer of the Day of Atonement, he speaks about the fear of being rejected or cheated by God, who either does or does not exist.

And tomorrow we shall die
without knowing why

Upon leaving we shall stand before a gate
and find it locked
Hearts which rejoiced:
God has gathered us!
Will doubt and tremble with fear

And if God does not exist, what then? Avraham Ben Yitzhak offers the glimmer of an answer:

A few may sing
Seven paths have led us astray
But upon one we shall return

When God is no longer with us, we only have each other. But "only" is not the right word; there is no need to mitigate it. We have each other. And if we have each other, then on the Day of Atonement we are responsible to forgive and forget.

As summer begins to withdraw and August begins to look like September, one hears a beautiful song in the streets of Jerusalem. The catchy tune is known by its first words, master of forgiveness, and it is an acrostic supplication to God, naming him as one steeped in justice and forgiveness, one who grants reprieve just one more time. The beautiful melody accompanying these words hails from the Jewish communities of the Middle East and is among the best known. I know most of it by heart, and so do many Jews who grew up in religious homes. I love it so much that it is one of the rare instances where I tried to maintain the syllabic count when I emended it, so that I could hum it when the time came. And come it did. I was so blessed when my composition was adopted by City Congregation as part of its liturgy for the High Holidays and two wonderfully talented vocalists sang it. I was blown away. It was the most meaningful liturgical experience of my life.

Freely Forgiving

Dearest companions you are:
Freely forgiving / Truly trusting
Deeply delving / Sincerely speaking

We have erred, cherished friends, please forgive us

Virtuously evaluating
Compassionately consoling
Unfailingly fulfilling
Courageously correcting

We have erred, cherished friends, please forgive us.[1]

This is my gift of tongues, my ability to create a synergy between English and Hebrew, and this poem is among the most brilliant jewels in my treasure chest.

יְקִירַי הֲלֹא אַתֶּם... [1]

אֱמוּנֵי הַסְּלִיחוֹת / בּוֹטְחֵי יְשָׁרוֹת / גּוֹלֵי עֲמוּקוֹת / דּוֹבְרֵי צְדָקוֹת
חָטָאנוּ חֲבֵרִים רַחֲמוּ עָלֵינוּ

הוֹגֵי יְשָׁרוֹת / וָתִיקֵי נֶחָמוֹת / זוֹכְרֵי בְרִיתוֹת / חוֹקְרֵי הַדּוֹרוֹת
חָטָאנוּ חֲבֵרוֹת רַחֲמוּ עָלֵינוּ

98

Part Three

Pontification

Introduction

You might suppose that as a rabbi and an erstwhile academic, I possess the gift of gab. After all, both these professions assume a certain predilection to loquacity. A successful rabbi should inspire with stirring sermons and galvanize his flock to conquer the citadel, or at least sponsor a refugee family from Afghanistan. Unfortunately, I lack the ability to successfully modulate my voice and that detracts from any speech I am wont to deliver. I can talk and talk and employ a wonderfully sophisticated vocabulary, but ultimately it is the garrulous gobble-gobble of a turkey rather than the galvanizing gab of an orator. Still, I have delivered some successful sermons in my time.

But how? The gift I have not mentioned, but which is, in a way, at the very root of who I am, is my self-awareness. I realized very early on in childhood that I didn't get it. And by "it," I mean many of the unwritten norms by which neurotypical people conducted themselves in the world.

Not that I needed much help understanding my lack of aptitude when it came to public speaking: My mother has told me my entire life that I don't get tone. Ironically, she would often level that criticism at me in a stentorian voice herself, but that doesn't mean it wasn't true.

And so I have, over the years, developed my own style of speaking. I always speak from the heart. There is no dissembling because I can't dissemble. And though I am still a relative novice at tone despite years of work, enough of my genuineness shines through that people can tell where I'm coming from. Thus, when I poke fun at myself, people know that in a profound way that self-deprecation is actually the truth, which makes it all the more funny. I can speak easily about deeply personal things, such as miscarriage and my child with special needs, because my sense of what is private is so very different than that of a neurotypical person, and I have come to realize that this is a great strength. When you share those type of moments with people, they will share with you in turn, and that is how you create community.

In the following section you will find some of the sermons I am proudest of, sermons that I felt stirred my audiences and sometimes galvanized them. I hope you think so too.

Rebuilding Compassion
Rosh Hashanah 2021

Our reservoirs of compassion have been sorely depleted in the past year. Mine too. My job as a rabbi partially depends on my ability to marshal my own feelings of concern for others and act empathetically. I still do, I am trying, but it is getting harder. Not because of the people of City Congregation—the members of my community have been great.

After one and a half years of a pandemic that has done its level best to separate us, we have stayed together.

It is getting harder because the world is such a troubled place and I feel so wind-tossed.

From many conversations I have had with members of my community and others, it is evident I am not the only one for whom compassion is more difficult.

I could urge you to try harder, but that is such a tired trope. We have all been trying hard.

Instead, throughout these High Holidays, I want to offer ways to replenish our reservoirs of compassion, to rebuild.

Years ago, at my ordination ceremony, Rabbi Adam Chalom gave me the best compliment ever. He said that he had never met anyone who was as deliberately kind as I am. He didn't give any examples that I recall; he may very well have been exaggerating. But he made me cry. No one had recognized this about me in the past. I had not even entirely articulated it to myself, but it is essential to who I am.

Because I am neurodivergent, there is a chasm between my understanding of the world and that of others. One of the ways I have sought to bridge that chasm is by being as kind as possible.

At the beginning, I would bungle this up too. Once someone dropped money on the bus, and I hurried to pick it up for them. They thought I was trying to steal it and reacted angrily. Another time, I was so voluble in my offers to help a young woman that she construed it as threatening and shied away from me.

But these days, I get it right more often.

Do I feel good inside when I act kindly? Sometimes, but more often, I don't.

Why is that? Shouldn't acts of kindness instill a fuzzy warm feeling in you, thus motivating you to do more of the same and making the world a better place? That would be awesome, and may be true for many people, including you, but so often it is not the case for me. It can be hard for me to interpret the feedback I receive, whether it is through body language or otherwise. When I do understand, it is great, but that is not the way it usually is. My deficits are considerable in this realm.

If someone smiles at me, I don't know if it is the grin of a lion about to pounce or the smile of a mother as she gazes at her child. Or the indulgent smiles that some of you are probably directing toward me or this page. Or more likely, the embarrassed smile of "ouch, he is blowing it."

But there is one thing that anchors me: my beliefs. And what I believe above all other things is that the principle of *love your neighbor as yourself* is critical to a smooth-running society, a society that cares. I say this from an entirely selfish perspective. I need help in this realm.

And so, I am very deliberate about my acts of kindness, despite not really knowing what the consequences of these acts are on others. I just hope beyond hope that just as I am kind to the world, the world will be kind to me.

And I have found it to be so. More often than not, people have been kind to me. Call me a deluded optimist, but I think the go-to of most of the communities I inhabit is kindness and care.

Take the horror of the pull-out from Afghanistan. Whatever one may think of the political justification of invading Afghanistan, staying there for a generation, and then leaving, a consistent thread I have noticed, on the left and on the right, is care. Care for the people who allied themselves with the Americans at considerable cost, and care for the last soldiers who remained in harm's way. Care for the people of Afghanistan, and especially the women, who would again have to endure a stringent form of Sharia law. This thread of caring is partially obfuscated by political posturing, but it is there. We as Americans, both on the right and the left, care, and that is so amazing to see.

You may counter and say, what you are proposing is so very basic. Of course, one should be kind on purpose, deliberately; that is the bedrock of ethics. But don't stop reading yet, that is not exactly what I am saying.

I am saying that whatever place or situation you find yourself in, especially mundane ones, or ones in which you are not inclined to think of ethics, you can ask yourself, "How can I make life just a little bit easier for someone else?"

When we see a person injured on the sidewalk, we run over and ask how they are doing and if we can call a doctor; this is straightforward, obvious. But in truth, in almost every situation in which we find ourselves in the world, there are ways to be nicer if we just take a moment to think about it.

A small example:

Whenever I enter a bus, I immediately think about the allocation of seats. I am hyper-analytic! I couldn't help it even if I tried.

I think about the people who are taking the outside seat, who make it harder for others who want or need to sit, unless they are willing to demand it. I see this as unfair. And so, often I don't take an open seat but rather endure the glare of the person who is hogging the row by requesting to sit in the inside seat, thus making it easier for a shy person to sit on the bus rather than stand.

This may seem so simple. But it is a situation wherein we don't usually think about kindness and ethics, and we can. For those of us who do this routinely, it can be helpful to remind ourselves that it actually is an act of kindness.

I've witnessed these deliberate acts of kindness at my congregation. At Shabbats when people gather and there is some quiet, which may feel awkward to some people, there is always someone who will step up and greet a guest, or comment on a nice outfit, or just say something about how beautiful the weather is. This may seem so small, but it is a deliberate act of making our shared environment more pleasant, and it is so important.

I believe with all my heart that when we engage in small acts of kindness habitually and purposely, we make the world a better place.

We make the world a better place when we step aside when someone is walking toward us on the sidewalk.

We make the world a safer place when we report poison ivy growing on the sidewalk of our neighborhood to 311.

We make the world more civil by offering politeness as a response to anger on social media or on Zoom.

And we make the world a kinder place when, if someone looks our way, we smile.

And since I am Canadian, I believe we make the world a more polite place by saying, I am sorry—even if it is not our fault.

The pandemic we are living in has taught us that we often have so little control over the arc of events that shape our lives. The one place where we have autonomy is our own actions, and we can choose to be kind. When the foundations of our life are in doubt, when nothing is certain, when we need to rebuild, we can be entirely deliberate about kindness, and it can become such a wonderful habit.

The Covid Test

September 2020

On so many days during the first two seasons of the pandemic, life seemed to fray at the seams.

I can't tell you how many times I felt like screaming—

—at the cashier at Rite Aid for not wearing a mask.

—at people not socially distancing at the grocery store.

—at my computer screen after hearing a stupid thing uttered by particular know-nothing politicians.

—at my wife for forgetting to pay a bill.

—at my son for reversing the contents of his plate onto the floor.

The reason for this rage is that the summer of 2020 was a summer of deep discontent permeating into every pore of our being. The United States is the richest country in the world, and yet we handled the COVID crisis so ineptly. Our caseload was the highest in the world. Our death rates were among the worst. And so many of our leaders willfully ignored science and pretended that the virus didn't and doesn't exist. The rest of the so-called first world countries left us behind; they managed to flatten the curve early and resume a quasi-normal life.

In 2020 I couldn't see my new nephew in Canada.

I couldn't celebrate a wedding in Israel.

I couldn't hug a friend who lost a father.

From this relatively sane corner of the United States, I gazed in horror at Florida and Texas and at the gross and criminal ineptitude of their leaders, and at individualism gone amok. COVID has tested us and we have seemingly failed the test. But we will have other chances.

One of the traditional readings at Rosh Hashanah is the story of Abraham's sacrifice of Isaac.

Seemingly out of nowhere, the God character of Genesis 22 commands Abraham to sacrifice his son Isaac on a mountain in the south. Abraham saddles his donkey, takes his young son, and goes into the desert. On the third day, they see the mountain in the distance. Abraham takes his son with him and they go up. Isaac asks his father, "I see the knife and the wood, but where is the sacrifice?" Abraham answers, "God will choose." On the mountain, Abraham places his son on the altar and binds him. And then he raises his knife...

American society is achingly situated at the point of this knife. Will we survive this crisis and become stronger for it, or will this devolution into anger continue to ravage us unabated?

I think we will come out stronger.

I think this because I have witnessed so many people rising to the occasion.

I saw such astonishing acts of selflessness by nurses and doctors, who cried in fear and despair, wiped their tears away, and tried to save another life.

I saw teachers work around the clock to try to teach children remotely, while they cared for their own families.

I saw delivery trucks driven by brave souls, distributing food to the ravaged population of New York City.

I saw my wife, who after a sleepless night with our baby, woke up to lead her community in song and greet another beautiful day full of death.

I saw all of this and I am filled with hope.

But what shall we do with our anger? What of the maskless man who invades our personal space in the middle of a virus wave and speaks of freedom?

Instead of kicking him, you could quote Mordecai Kaplan's ethical aphorism to him: *The indulgence in freedom unrestrained by self-discipline is intrinsically the source of conflict.*

But for some reason, I don't think that will be particularly effective.

In mid-July of 2020 I read an article in the *New York Times* about how one doctor tried to understand the motivations of the maskless. She truly tried to listen, and having heard, tried to effect change. She got thousands of responses and was a force for good.

Maskless behavior through one lens is reckless and is indicative of a complete lack of empathy toward others.

Viewed through another lens, it is a coping mechanism against the powerlessness we feel toward this virus that has upended our lives. "I am not afraid of the virus, therefore I will not wear a mask."

That person may not believe that there is anything they can do to prevent community spread, so why should they wear a mask?

That person may believe that since they have already been sick with COVID they no longer spread the virus.

111

Or that person may believe that the virus is fake and that Fauci is the antichrist.

There is a valuable discussion and debate to be had regarding individuality versus collectivism. At what point does our individuality, our right to choose the proper path for ourselves, infringe too greatly upon the greater good? If we don't have these debates, if we don't grant our maskless fellow due consideration, if we label that person with a pejorative, we exacerbate and inflame the horrible tensions that already exist in our society.

We must listen. We must see the other as valuable, even as we are balanced upon this knife. It is so hard.

Back to the story of sacrifice. Abraham raised his knife. At this point there are two versions of the story. In one version Abraham kills Isaac; in another version an angel stops him.

Both versions of the story are horrible.

Any and all orders to kill are horrible.

The situation we are in is horrible.

But in the second version of the story Isaac is saved, and that version of the story, highlighting the value of human life, is the one that wins out.

I believe with all my heart that we will win our many battles against COVID, and that we will come out stronger. I believe that we will win the fight against intolerance, against systemic racism, against those who seek to divide and inflame.

And the numbers support this. At first blush it may not seem that way, because of the existence of such horrible inflammatory rhetoric. But they do.

The United States is a less racist country than it has ever been. Survey after survey confirm that this is true. Mississippi, the state that is emblematic of the Deep South, took down its Confederate flag in 2020. It took them only 150 years or so, but they did it.

It is no longer legal to discriminate against people at work on the basis of their sexual orientation. That is amazing, and the majority 6-3 opinion of the Supreme Court was authored by none other than Neil Gorsuch.

Deep and very painful conversations about privilege are occurring in every corner of our society, and marginalized groups are leading this dialogue. While there has been an inevitable backlash, I find this nothing short of incredible.

In the middle of the pandemic, as I looked at the devastation around me, I told myself through the tears that this too shall pass, and we shall come out stronger. I still believe this to be true.

Difference

Rosh Hashanah 2019

In August of 2019, I was arrested at a protest against the horrendous immigration policies being enacted in the United States. I was arrested on a Jewish fast day with 43 other clergy and activists after staging a sit-in at the Amazon bookstore. The most heartrending part of our sit-in was when the names of refugees who died in American custody were read out loud. So many of us were in tears.

These people were the quintessential others, and they are no longer with us.

This moment began a process for me, a process in which I thought about the concept of "the other" and how I as an individual and we as a community could improve in our treatment of others.

Who is the other? The other is definitely the refugee, the downtrodden, but more expansively, the other is everybody, or everyone "else." The others are our parents and our children, our spouses and our closest friends.

As much as we seek to understand someone else, even someone very close to us, can we truly get there? Can we truly understand someone else's inner life?

We make assumptions that others share our premises, share our worldview, share our opinions, but so often we are wrong. Because of this, as parents, as children, as friends, sometimes we make mistakes, horrible mistakes that we can never completely rectify. Can we forgive ourselves? Can I forgive myself?

I want to share with you two interactions with my son and my father—interactions where my weaknesses led to destructive outcomes.

My beautiful five-year-old son Elisha is my spitting image. He looks like me, has the same allergies I had growing up, is introverted, and is an auditory learner. I thought I saw a mirror of myself. We so often see our children in this way.

Elisha is named for one of the great Jewish heretics of 1800 years ago, Elisha ben Abuyah. According to legend, Elisha had a life-altering experience that caused him to doubt whether a benevolent overseeing God existed. He abandoned mainstream Judaism and was vilified in horrible ways by every subsequent generation of Jews. One of the greatest rabbinic sages became the quintessential Other. In fact, throughout rabbinic literature, he is simply referred to as *acher*, "different" or "other" in Hebrew. I named my son Elisha because I wished to honor this great man for bravely saying what others did not. My beautiful Elisha is not "the other" in this way. He was born to parents who love him deeply and care for him as best they know how. He has a gentle older brother, two other siblings he loves, and caring grandparents and relatives. He is lucky in this way.

When Elisha was three, he stopped speaking. He withdrew from the daily routine at his nursery, and no amount of prodding by his teachers or his parents convinced him to join, to play, to be a child.

Instead of addressing this immediately, I just assumed that he was like me as a child, that he was withdrawing and assessing, learning. He wasn't. He was an other, a different person than me, and his withdrawal was entirely different than mine, and very serious. I waited a year until we sought therapy. My little Elisha lost a year of his childhood that I will never be able to give back to him because I could not recognize that he was different than me and I didn't know what was best for him. We have fought the Department of Education tooth and nail for him to receive services that he needs, and he is making progress, but it is so very hard to forgive myself for the year he lost.

A second horrible mistake I made, of a very different type, was with my father about five months ago. I love my father, but we fight a lot. With all the rest of the world, I am patient, I am very slow to anger, but not with him. I always feel that he should know better.

I underwent one of the hardest times in my life at the beginning of 2019. In January 2019, we lost one of the twins we were supposed to have, and a very high-risk pregnancy ensued. In the midst of this personal hardship, one of my solaces was writing and poetry. I had just finished my Haggadah, which I was really proud of. A friend who had adopted Judaism eight years ago read the Haggadah throughout the Seder. It was the only time I had seen him read a Jewish book with such focus. He really liked it. Then my father got his talons into my Haggadah and eviscerated it, claiming that I had actually written a supersessionist Christian work and that it was about as worthwhile as toilet paper. This was two weeks before my son Nadav was born in an emergency C-section that may have saved his life, so I was in one of the most vulnerable places, poised on the aching precipice of powerlessness and despair, and my father was entirely oblivious to this. He was entirely oblivious that there is a time and a place to deliver serious criticism.

I blew up at him, and we had the worst fight of our lives. I told him exactly what I thought about his behavior, and it wasn't pretty.

I regret this deeply. I have given my father other works to look at since as a peacemaking gesture, since intellectual exchange is at the core of our interactions, but our relationship has taken a bad hit.

So where does that leave me?

"To err is human," you may say, but I would answer, "to forgive is divine," and since I am not a god, I haven't forgiven myself for either of these episodes.

What I have done is thought very deeply about the bedrock of our ethics: Love your neighbor as yourself. I'd always thought that what it meant was be polite, show empathy, and be kind. I have tried to live this way, not always successfully. Now I realize that treating others the way you would like to be treated should be refined in a very important way. Ideally, we should be treating others the way *they themselves* would like to be treated, and it is so very hard to know what that means even when we are very close to people. I should have realized that Elisha was not me. I should have realized that perhaps my father was trying to create a veneer of normality under extraordinarily difficult conditions. Perhaps he was so very worried himself. I didn't. I let anger wash over me.

118

It is so very hard to understand others. We can try and we should try, but we will inevitably fail quite a bit.

Knowing this, realizing our ignorance, I think the best posture is to assume the best motivations of people. Assuming the best even when we are wrong, and we are wrong often, has the potential to elevate others. Yes, we will be hurt, sometimes badly, but in the end the world becomes a better place, a place with more goodwill, and that is one of the central goals of humanism, which is my philosophy.

My Love Letter to City Congregation

(Or my job talk, if you prefer)
April 2018

Love poetry!

Love poetry is perhaps my favorite form of literary expression. I've written dozens and dozens of such poems, to my dearest love Aviva, to my beautiful children, to sorely missed friends and relatives who are no longer among the living.

I want to offer you a short tasting menu of Jewish love poetry throughout the ages. I will present compositions from the dawn of history, culminating in poems written only a few months ago. Some of these poems are meant to be recited and some are meant to be sung, for as my friend sometimes says, a poem without a tune is like a body without a soul—though, to be fair, we humanists don't really believe in souls. I will do this first in the original language of composition (at least a bit of it), so as to give you a more authentic feel for the composition, and then in translation.

After I present these poems, I will talk about the authors and give you a little background to the compositions and ask two basic questions. What makes them Jewish compositions? And what is the appeal of this poetry then and now?

Peace Be Still

I will begin with the simplest composition, "Peace Be Still." This is the first song I sang to my son Lev, who was born seven weeks early. I sang this as I looked at him in his incubator at the NICU at NYU Langone hospital. I could not even touch him to offer him comfort after being torn out early from his mother's womb; he was too small and fragile. My heart was broken, and this began my process of healing.

PEACE BE STILL
(unknown author, 20th century)

Peace be still and know that you are loved
Peace be still and know that you are
Peace be still and know
Peace be still
Peace be
Peace Peace Peace

Though this song is essentially only nine words long, it resonates with allusions to Jewish literature. I don't know who composed the tune or the specific lyrics, but the cadences are biblical. According to the Exodus myth, the Israelites stood by the Reed Sea and were told to be still and watch the raging sea be calmed. Their sea was my raging heart; I wasn't only singing the song to Lev, I was singing it to myself. Though we as humanists do not believe that the Exodus myth actually occurred, we acknowledge that is an important one in the history of the world, informing the liberation stories from countless tyrannies throughout the ages.

Here I was trying to liberate myself from the small-scale tyranny of the medical establishment that had pulled my son out before his time. Though I don't know who composed it, I relate to it expansively as Jewish, in consideration of this mythical resonance.

The Love Song of Shu-Sin

After this prelude (be charitable when you imagine my off-key singing), let us begin our journey throughout history. It starts 4000 years ago, with "The Love Song of Shu-Sin," a king in Mesopotamia or Iraq who wrote—in Sumerian—the following hymn for his Goddess in her voice. Here I bring a few excerpts, and I will speak below about the translator.

> Bridegroom, dear to my heart,
> Goodly is your beauty, honeysweet...
> You have captivated me, let me stand tremblingly before you.
> Bridegroom, I would be taken by you to the bedchamber...
> My precious caress is more savory than honey,
> In the bedchamber, honey-filled,
> Let me enjoy your goodly beauty...
> Your heart, I know where to gladden your heart,
> Lion, sleep in our house until dawn.

This is the first love song we have a record of. Considering its artful form, it is likely that many love songs preceded it, yet they are lost in time. This is seemingly not a Jewish love poem. It was written more than 4000 years ago, and there were no Jews or Israelites then. And it was written in Sumerian, not a Jewish or even a Semitic language. Yet it would have remained hidden among the hundreds of thousands of tablets in the dustbins of a museum were it not for the great Jewish scholar Samuel Noah Kramer, who translated it.[2] This is a poem about a king in love with his goddess. This goddess was obviously flesh and blood, for there was a tradition in the temples of the East that the king and the chief priestess would join together in sexual coupling as representatives of male and female deities. There is a mutuality, a love between equals, that continues to reverberate through compositions, despite the sexism, despite the hierarchies, despite the rigid patriarchies of ancient times. This makes love poetry unique among ancient literary compositions.

---

[2] Samuel Noah Kramer, *History Begins at Sumer*, 246-247.

The Love Song of the Shepherdess

The first Jewish love songs are found in our omnibus of myth, the Bible, in a book called the Song of Songs. No one knows for sure when this book was written, maybe 500 BCE. This book is unique in the context of the Bible; God doesn't exist there, it celebrates human love.

I am a rose of Sharon,
a lily of the valleys.
As a lily among brambles,
so is my love among maidens.
As an apple tree among the trees of the wood,
so is my beloved among young men.
With great delight I sat in his shadow,
and his fruit was sweet to my taste.
He brought me to the banqueting house,
and his intention toward me was love.
Sustain me with raisins,
refresh me with apples;
for I am faint with love.
O that his left hand were under my head,
and that his right hand embraced me!

I adjure you, O daughters of Jerusalem,
    by the gazelles or the wild does:
    do not stir up or awaken love
        until it is ready!

The female is imagined as a lily among the thorns; the male lover as an apple tree with sweet fruit. The female lover asks for an apple. They are in a garden, or perhaps *the* Garden, for in love poetry throughout the Western world, we are often transported to the first mythic love of Adam and Eve in the Garden of Eden.

Ben Sira's Ode to Wisdom

Now we skip a few hundred years into the future to Jerusalem in the year 200 BCE. The Greeks, led by Alexander the Great, have conquered much of the world, and their culture has permeated the region. Shimon Ben Sira, a sage who lived in Jerusalem of that age, was a man very much affected by the Hellenistic ethos of education yet fiercely proud of his heritage. He composed the following love song to Wisdom:

> From blossom to ripening grape
> my heart delighted in her;
> my foot entered upon the straight path;
> from my youth I followed her steps.
> I inclined my ear a little and received her,
> and I found for myself much instruction.
> I made progress therein;
> to him who teaches wisdom I will give glory.
> For I resolved to live according to wisdom,
> and I was zealous for the good;
> and I shall never be put to shame.
> My soul grappled with wisdom,
> and in my conduct I was strict;
> I spread out my hands to the sky,
> and lamented my ignorance of her.

I directed my soul to her,
and through purification I found her.
I gained understanding with her from the first,
therefore I will not be forsaken.
My heart was stirred to seek her,
therefore I have gained a good possession.

Ben Sira imagined wisdom to be his seductress, whom he followed in his youth, never looking back. Wisdom is not only his equal, she is his superior; this is deeply ironic because Ben Sira was one of the most deeply misogynistic writers of the Jewish literary canon, valuing submissiveness and seeing daughters as unfortunate burdens rather than human beings. This is another example of love poetry being a powerful equalizer, overcoming the patriarchy and societal norms to be an effective motivator.

Saul's Ode to Love

Skipping forward in time to another part of the world, a man known to Christians as Paul and to Jews as Saul of Tarsus writes a love poem. Like the atheist Song of Songs, his love poem from I Corinthians is unique in the New Testament. It's a poem about 'agape', love as an attribute, and not a poem to any particular individual. (I read this in the original Greek to impress my audience, but there is no Greek here!)

Love is patient; love is kind; love is not
envious or boastful or arrogant or rude.
It does not insist on its own way; it is not
irritable or resentful; it does not rejoice in
wrongdoing, but rejoices in the truth.
It bears all things, believes all things, hopes all
things, endures all things.
Love never ends.
But as for prophecies, they will come to an
end; as for tongues, they will cease; as for
knowledge, it will come to an end....
And now faith, hope, and love abide, these
three; and the greatest of these is love.

What I take from this poem is that love is different things for different people, but all acknowledge love's power. This is a beautiful sentiment, but how is it Jewish? Well, Saul or Paul was a Jew writing to Jews (and others) and about Jews. His writing became the basis of a new religion about 200 years later, but as a Jewish sage once said, love blurs all boundaries, so let us include these idealistic words in the canon of Jewish love poetry.

Yehudah Halevi's Love for Shabbat and for Men

Love can be between people, but also for a particular food or even for a day of the week. Yehudah Halevi loved Saturday— or Shabbat—and wrote it a spicy love song. He lived in the 11th and 12th centuries in the golden age of the intersection between Christian, Muslim, and Jewish culture in Spain. He was very conscientious about meter, and so this was put to song many times. (Once again please imagine me singing a snippet here in the original Hebrew, but this time imagine me singing well, because this is a piece that I love dearly.)

The six days are your faithful slaves
Though I work, it is you that I crave
Only a few days away
and then we will play

How I yearn for the time
between sun and moon
Guests arriving so soon
I will serve them apples and wine

O Shabbes, come under my Tallis
We're about to have fun
Three times my love, I did promise

Yehudah Halevi wasn't just spicy about his love for Shabbat; he was very honest about his homosexual relationships. This may seem very progressive for the 11-12th century, but in fact homosexuality was culturally known and accepted to varying degrees among the intellectual elites influenced by Greek mores. Here is one of the love songs he wrote about the yearning he felt for his narcissistic paramour which I translated from the original Hebrew.

When we were enjoying ourselves
as he sat upon my knees
He saw his image reflected in my eyes
and so he kissed them
But he was kissing his own reflection
and not me

He asked what is wrong
with my magnificent buck,
why are your eyes so red
I answered these eyes kill my love,
and what you see is blood,

As a deer is devoured,
so he devoured my heart
Weak in my thighs, his heart so obdurate
I asked him please,
but he would not let me go,
and snatched my soul away
He kissed me, and I turned to go,
but my spirit is diminished in yearning

for another day
And as I pass through his garden
my heart melts and runs
As though his gate, were the gate to perdition,
and my soul already gone

So many of us have experienced love's anguish, and so did Yehudah Halevi 1000 years ago. He was infatuated with a narcissistic but beautiful younger man, and he realized that he should break off the relationship, but not before his heart was broken. We have read about love's sweetness, its passion, and now the pain.

Yearning to Be a Woman: Kalonymus ben Kalonymus

In 14ᵗʰ-century Provence, Kalonymus, the son of Kalonymus, advisor to kings, a rabbi, and a poet loved the idea of becoming a woman. This is one of the only poems in ancient Jewish sources that speaks of this particular anguish and yearning, and it is definitely the most explicit of them. Here are some excerpts of his long poem, though one is not entirely sure if "his" is the pronoun Kalonymus would have preferred.

> What a tragedy for my mother
> that she bore a boy.
> How worthless! . . .
> Let the one who announced to my father:
> "It's a boy!" . . . be cursed
>
> Had the craftsman who created me
> made me a proper woman,
> today I would be discerning and wise,
> a weaver of yarns.
>
> My sisters and I would grasp the loom and tell
> each other stories of light and darkness.

What I wouldn't give if you transformed me
from a man into a woman
Were I only to have merited this, being so
graced by your goodness. . .
But what is there to say,
though I cry and am bitter
For my father in heaven gave his decree
and maimed me immutably

Some have interpreted this poem as satirical—since it can be
so hard to imagine this experience in the 14th century
(Kalonymus did write satire). But after reading it multiple
times, I want to see it as genuine. There is too much raw
emotion here to understand it otherwise. And there is little
doubt that transgenderism is as old as time.

Primavera en Salonika

More than five hundred years ago the Jews were expelled from Spain and then Portugal upon pain of death. The Sephardi Jews spread all over Europe and beyond to North America, establishing new communities everywhere they went. One of the jewels of the Jewish world was the community in Salonika, Greece, where they spoke Judeo-Spanish or Ladino. Here is a snippet of a folk song about spring in Salonika. It is sung beautifully by Savina Yannatou in her collection of Sephardi folk songs:[3]

PRIMAVERA EN SALONIKA

Allí al café Maslum
Una niña de ojos pretos
Que canta y sona ud

No me manques, tú Fortuna
Del café de Avrám Maslúm
Tú quitas los muestros dertes
Que cantas y sonas ud

---

[3] Savina Yannatou, *Anoixi Sti Saloniki*, 2008.

Springtime in Salonika

At Maslum's Café
There is a young woman with mysterious eyes
Who sings, accompanied by her oud

Forget me not, O Fortuna
At Abram Maslum's Café
You banish our grief
With your songs accompanied by an oud

This poem, composed in the early 20th century, evokes the cosmopolitan yet mysterious flavor of this city to the haunting sounds of a young woman playing the oud, a Mediterranean stringed instrument. They meet at Abram Maslum's café and she scorches him with her eyes—such was Salonika in the late 19th and early 20th century. This is a love song to a place that no longer exists, and when read or sung today, there is a layer of nostalgia and sadness for the vibrant Jewish communities of yesteryear, which were destroyed in the Holocaust of the mid-20th century.

I Don't Believe in Heaven

Heinrich Heine was one of the most important German poets of the 19th century. He was born Jewish but was a reluctant convert to Christianity in order to gain acceptance into the academy and in wider circles, though that didn't entirely work out for him. He is famous for saying on his deathbed that he never really left Judaism. Here is a love poem composed while he was sitting in church daydreaming.

ICH GLAUBE NICHT

Ich glaub' nicht an den Himmel,
Wovon das Pfäfflein spricht;
Ich glaub' nur an dein Auge,
Das ist mein Himmelslicht.

Ich glaub' nicht an den Herrgott,
Wovon das Pfäfflein spricht;
Ich glaub' nur an dein Herze,
'nen andern Gott hab' ich nicht.

Ich glaub' nicht an den Bösen,
An Höll' und Höllenschmerz;
Ich glaub' nur an dein Auge,
Und an dein böses Herz.

I DON'T BELIEVE

I don't believe in the sky above
Of which the pastor writes
I believe only in your eyes, my love
They are my heavenly light

I do not believe in God almighty
Of which my pastors preach
I believe only in your heart
No other, I beseech

I do not believe in evil
Or in hell's trials and travails
I believe in your eyes, my devil
And in your heart's wiles

Like many Jews throughout time, Heine sought acceptance but found it hard to find, both among the intellectual elites in Paris and also in his relationships. Heine believed in humans, not in God, like us. But here is the twist: Humans betrayed him too, and thus he finds the devil in his love's eyes, and ultimately no salvation there either.

Katyusha

We now move to the 20th century and its great upheavals. The Jews were among the greatest believers in the communist experiment that wracked much of Asia and that continues to reverberate to this very day with Russia's invasion of Ukraine. One of the most famous love poems, "Katyusha," was written by two small towners (Matvey Blanter and Mikhail Isakovsky), one of them Jewish (Blanter), who received the Order of Lenin for their efforts. (I sang the first verse in the original Russian, to impress my audience, but I shall spare you and not transcribe it here.)

> Apple trees and pears were blossoming,
> Fog was drifting upon the river.
> Katyusha strode out upon the shores,
> Upon the steep and lofty shores.
>
> She was strolling, singing a song
> About a great bird of the plains,
> About her true love,
> Whose missives she was keeping.

The same pastoral scenes one finds in the Song of Songs are found here, except here, later in the song, Katyusha's love for her soldier competes with his love for the Motherland. In the end, both endure. The poem emphasizes that she is just an ordinary girl, an ordinary girl whose walk on the riverbank in the spring is one of the most famous poems ever translated from Russian. When one is in love, suddenly every little thing your lover does is so meaningful: every gesture, every glance, every silence.

If You Didn't Exist

Joe Dassin was an American exile who ended up in Paris. His parents left Hollywood after the infamous communist purges in the middle of last century. He wandered the boulevards of Paris in search of true love, of an ideal, and his heart was broken after the death of his first son, barely born. Here is a snippet of one his most famous songs, "Et Si Tu N'Existais Pas" ("If You Didn't Exist").

Et si tu n'existais pas,
Dis-moi pourquoi j'existerais.
Pour traîner dans un monde sans toi,
Sans espoir et sans regrets…

If you didn't exist
Tell me why should I?
Why should I slog through the world
Without hope and without regrets

Dassin sang some of the most famous French chansons of last century. In this haunting song, the idea of mutuality is elevated: One soul cannot exist without another. A famous compendium of Jewish proverbs from the 2nd century, *Wisdom of the Fathers,* says that if I am not for myself, then who is, and if not now, when? It may be that this maxim inspired this song. Dassin, after all, (probably) went to Hebrew school.

Tumbalalaika

If there is one Yiddish love song that people know, it is "Tumbalalaika," wherein a young man tries to find out who is the wittiest lass of them all and asks a few riddles:

Meidl Meidl,
Ikh veel bei ihr fregen
Vus ken vaksen, vaksen on regen
Vus ken brenen un nit oifhern
Vus ken veynen benken on treren

Tumbala, Tumbala, Tumbalalaika
Tumbala, Tumbala, Tumbalalaika
Tumbalalaika, strum balalaika
Tumbalalaika, may we be happy

Girl, girl, I want to ask of you
What can grow, grow without rain?
What can burn and never end?
What can yearn, cry without tears?

Foolish lad, why do you have to ask?
A stone can grow, grow without rain
Love can burn and never end
A heart can yearn, cry without tears

The climax of this love song is "what can burn and never stop burning?" The answer, of course, is love. The idea of love burning is one of those constants, existing in the earliest love poetry until this very day. This love song seemingly answers all the riddles—or does it? We don't know if the lass snared the boy or not.

My Heart Is My Guide

Leila Mourad was an Egyptian singer and actress of the mid 20th century. She was the daughter of a famous Jewish cantor at a time when it was becoming difficult to be Jewish in Egypt, yet Mourad became so famous that in the canon of Egyptian singers, she was second only to Umm Kulthum. Like Heine, she paid a steep price: As anti-Zionist fervor engulfed Egypt, she felt her only recourse was to convert to Islam. Her family renounced her, and after one of her films was boycotted she didn't act or sing again. This is one of her most famous songs: "Ana Albi Dalili" ("My Heart Is My Guide").

My heart is my guide,
It told me that I would fall in love with you
It always speaks to me, and I believe my heart
My heart is my guide, my heart is my guide
My love is here with me even before I see him

. . . .

I hear him, oh he says to me
O love come here, come here, come here

The Kiss

And here we are in the 21st century. Julie Enszer is a wonderfully explicit and evocative poet who is one of my windows into exclusively female relationships. Most notably she is the editor of a collection of Jewish lesbian poetry, *Milk and Honey*. She has a gift of elegantly yet simply relating deep truths. She reminds me of Yehuda Amichai in this respect, which is one of the highest compliments I can pay to a poet. Here are a few snippets of one of the poems in the aforementioned collection. This is the only poem I've ever seen which actually mentions hemorrhoids.

> The easy embrace of these two lovers
> the way their arms fit perfectly
> around the other
> the same height
> their lips and eyes meet exactly....

> This is what I despise about poems—
> the way they isolate
> distill life to only the good parts
> they never capture this—
> our need
> for hemorrhoidal creams, shady lawyers,
> and breakfast cereals fortified with fiber

The line that strikes me most is the following: "This is what I despise about poems—the way they isolate distill life to only the good parts." I sometimes hate this too, yet I didn't realize it until I read Enszer's poem. This is the flip side of the idealization that one finds in love poetry—the hemorrhoidal cream, as it were.

Come My Tzaddik

But let us return for one final moment to ideals as we arrive at the present day and the work of a little-known poet, Tzemah Yoreh (yours truly). He wrote this song to his love Aviva in memory of so many beautiful walks by bodies of water and so many beautiful songs she sang to him and with him throughout the years of their courtship and marriage.

Come my righteous one
Let us walk on the paths
By the river
On Shabbat eve
There's a secret place
No one knows about it
I prepared us a dinner by candlelight
Shall two companions walk together if it wasn't written?
My pillar, my comfort, I did not light the candles
I wait for your kiss to ignite the fire
And together we will fill the world
With the light of our creation.

Conclusion

The final chapter of this book was a love letter to my congregation: It was with that speech that I wooed them, and it was based on these words, which I delivered on three separate occasions, that they agreed to hire me. I see that love letter as more reflective of my relationship with City Congregation than the contract I later signed.

But what happens when the honeymoon is over, and you are suddenly in over your head in a long-term relationship?

Not so many years ago, I was walking down a Jerusalem boulevard with a friend of mine on the Day of Atonement, the central fast day of the Jewish calendar. We had just finished the traditional afternoon prayers, which I find particularly meaningless, considering that at that point on the fast day, all I can think of is food. It was sweltering hot.

I had mostly been able to avoid going to synagogue that year, but considering my wife's position in her community, I had to be seen, as it were, and I had chosen the shortest of the five rounds of prayer to attend.

If this tableau had been captured on camera, the title would have been "futility." Actually, though, it was a turning point in my life, though I didn't know it at the time.

As we were walking together, my friend Jane and I were having a languorous chat about careers. Those conversations always left me depressed because of the nagging feeling that I wasn't doing enough with my own life. My biggest accomplishment in the past year had been synchronizing my three-year-old's and my baby's nap.

I am not kidding.

Jane's husband was a reform rabbi in the southern United States. He was a brilliant and gregarious man and was about one year away from quitting. So many congregational rabbis quit, but I didn't know at the time why that was the case. The pay is good, and the hours are flexible. It wasn't clear to me then that being a congregational rabbi can sometimes take a bite of your soul.

It must have been the heat, but for the first time an idea bubbled out of my fermented mind. I told Jane that I too was considering rabbi-ing as a career.

After all, I technically had the title.

She was taken aback for a moment and she laughed so hard she almost rolled on the ground. She thought I was telling a joke.

Jane knew me, or thought she did, and clearly could not conceive of someone who couldn't handle benign dinner conversations navigating the treacherous terrain of schmoozing. Every pastor knows you gotta schmooze. I was also fairly well-known as an out-of-the-closet atheist, so it's not as if most communities would bend over backward to hire me. I wasn't quite insulted by Jane's laughter, because there was more than a dollop of truth in her assessment. But I have never liked people telling me I was incapable of something.

And then a few months later, I saw an ad for this rabbi job online, and I was primed to try my luck, because Jane had laughed.

I bemusedly advanced through the interview process, never imagining that my candidacy would be taken seriously. I mean really! What business did a person with my profile and perceived deficits have applying for a leadership position? I couldn't even schmooze! To their great credit, the search committee saw something more, something I did not, and I got the job.

When the going got tough, and it did, I remembered the conversation with Jane many times. My first summer, I met with forty or fifty congregants at their homes, at restaurants, at bars, and got to know them. I basically did more interacting with human beings than I had in the decade beforehand; forty first dates. And my headaches were horrible.

But this passed, and before I knew it the first year had passed too, and I was doing fine. The learning curve was over. I had proven to Jane that I could do the rabbi thing and I was proud of myself. I was an autistic man doing something very unexpected and perhaps remarkable with my life.

But now that I had faced the challenge, I had to ask myself whether I had taken the job for the right reasons and whether I should continue. Considering the tone of this book, and the messages herein, you may expect a positive answer to these questions. But actually, the answer is mixed.

Taking a job because you need to prove something to yourself and not because the job suits you is not a wise course in life. I know, for example, that I would do well as an accountant. I am a whiz at numbers and their manipulation. But I would find the job stultifying. I'd probably try to get creative, and if you're a creative accountant, you may end up on the wrong side of lady law and land in a very bad place.

That does not necessarily mean that now that I've decided to be a rabbi, the job can't grow on me. It did. I helped infuse people's lives with meaning, and there is nothing more important than that. I feel a deep sense of satisfaction knowing that. And yet many aspects of rabbi-ing are essentially logistic: creating bar mitzvah booklets, managing events, running a Sunday School—jobs that I *can* do, but that other people can do better (on certain days, I would venture to say much better).

And what happens when there is burnout, as is true in communities all over the country? COVID is still with us and sometimes people have so little to give. I feel responsible, I feel I am failing somehow, even if that is probably not the objective truth.

What should I do then? Should I pack my bags? Too many rabbis and pastors in too many communities have done so. I would not leave my congregation in the lurch! I've invested too much time and energy in my community's success to leave. There is an important bond here. It is not just another job. I am a loyal spouse and father, and I am a loyal congregational leader. Even though it started as a dare, I am invested in succeeding.

But.

But I have to make my job work for me. I need to create a balance that is sustainable for the long term. I need to do more of what I love doing: more writing, more teaching, more talking from the heart, more reaching people on a personal level wherever they may be, so that I can thrive.

I have been completely honest with my congregation about this. We are in it together, and if that means shifting what it means to be a rabbi of a community, if that means becoming

154

an accommodating group, embracing the neurodivergent among us and understanding that they are worthy members and leaders, we accept the challenge.

Jewish humanism is deliberately untraditional, and that is part of our strength. In this third year of the pandemic, so many communities are being forced to reimagine themselves, their leadership structures, the way they meet, how they answer the needs of their members. We can too. There is nothing more important.

Please wish us luck.

Made in the USA
Middletown, DE
22 December 2022

20156873R00091